English
for
academic
study:

Speaking

Teacher's Book

Joan McCormack and Sebastian Watkins

University of
Reading

CALS

Centre for
Applied Language Studies

Garnet
EDUCATION

Credits

Published by
Garnet Publishing Ltd.
8 Southern Court
South Street
Reading RG1 4QS, UK

First published 2007
Fully revised 2009

ISBN: 978 1 85964 500 0

British Library Cataloguing-in-Publication Data
A catalogue record for this book is available from the
British Library.

Production

Project manager:	Simone Davies
Project consultant:	Rod Webb
Editorial team:	Penny Analytis, Simone Davies, Fiona McGarry, Nicky Platt
Art director:	Mike Hinks
Design and layout:	Sarah Church

Every effort has been made to trace copyright holders
and we apologize in advance for any unintentional
omissions. We will be happy to insert the appropriate
acknowledgements in any subsequent editions.

Printed and bound in Lebanon by International Press

Contents

Book map

Topic	Skills focus	Language focus
1 Communicating in academic situations	• Delivering a presentation	• Reporting back on a discussion • Agreeing and disagreeing • Using signpost expressions
2 Seminars and discussions	• Recognizing different perspectives • Reaching a balanced conclusion	• Comparing perspectives • Summarizing the outcome of a discussion • Chairing a discussion
3 Examining underlying assumptions	• Presenting information from a text • Anticipating arguments before a discussion	• Referring to a text • Exchanging opinions
4 Reading into speaking	• Using a text to support your ideas • Listening actively • Exchanging information (1)	• Clarifying and confirming understanding
5 The use of data	• Presenting information from charts • Building on what others have said	• Referring to data • Referring to what previous speakers have said
6 Consolidation unit	• Leading a seminar	• Review and consolidation
7 Supporting your point of view	• Finding a focus for a presentation • Preparing for a discussion by thinking the issues through	• Taking turns in a discussion
8 Collecting and presenting data	• Designing a questionnaire • Participating in a debate	• Expressing quantity
9 Thinking rationally	• Presenting a research proposal	• Expressing doubt/belief
10 The importance of reflection	• Exchanging information (2)	• Review and consolidation

Introduction

Principles

Skills development

A needs analysis based on questionnaires completed by international students in various departments of the University of Reading shows that participating in seminar discussions and giving formal presentations remain the two most common forms of oral communication that students engage in on their academic courses. Students, therefore, need instruction and repeated practice in these two complex skills.

Language focus

English for Academic Purposes (EAP) students need practice in applying the language they already have at their disposal in different oral academic situations. They also need to extend their grammatical, lexical and functional range through an explicit focus on language items.

Reflective learning

Learning should accelerate when the learner takes responsibility for being actively involved in the process. Students need to engage in an ongoing process of reflection on their performance and progress in key oral skills. Self-assessment is part of the process of fostering learner autonomy; by getting students constantly to think about their performance and how it can be improved, as well as being more aware of the progress they are hopefully making.

Feedback

Learners need feedback to help them move forward. In addition to self-assessment, students can benefit from peer evaluation. In peer evaluation, students can focus on particular skills, e.g., those involved in seminars and presentations. However, it is essential that the teacher, as language expert, also provides feedback on language performance.

Critical thinking

Content used on EAP courses needs to be stimulating and challenging enough to allow for the development of critical thinking skills. The topics and tasks, as in other components of the course, encourage and develop this essential aspect of academic study, challenging students to look at issues from a range of perspectives.

Reading into speaking

On their academic courses, students are continually reading and responding to written texts. These texts inform their written work, as well as their output in seminars and presentations. Students, therefore, need practice in responding orally to written texts, either as sources of information to support points made or as a stimulus to their own thinking.

Scaffolded learning

Learners need to be given more support in the earlier stages of the learning process. As learners progress through a course, the level of input and guidance can be gradually reduced, pushing students to respond to the challenge of operating independently.

How the materials relate to the principles

Skills development

Seminar skills

The materials encourage learners to become active participants in group discussions. In addition to skills such as managing a discussion and fostering group dynamics, there is an emphasis on the following interrelated areas:

- **Active listening skills**
  This is important as some students have a tendency to focus on what they want to say, rather than listening properly to the current speaker and responding appropriately.

- **Building on what the previous speaker has said**
  An effective group discussion should involve a series of linked interactions, rather than a collection of unrelated turns, thus moving the discussion forward.

- **Interlocutor skills**
  This involves responding to a turn by querying or challenging the speaker in a way which obliges her/him to clarify or expand on a point. This type of questioning helps take the discussion forward, and this is typical of academic interchange.

The above points reflect the ideas of Basturkmen (2002), who advocates a greater emphasis on the 'negotiation of ideas' in EAP spoken language materials. She contrasts a static view of discussion where speakers express pre-formed ideas, with a more dynamic view in which ideas emerge through the process of interaction. In the latter, participants modify, refine, and clarify their thinking through a collaborative process. Discourse and meaning are co-constructed. When an interlocutor expresses dissatisfaction with a response and pushes a peer to a more in-depth answer, this drives the discussion forward and leads to the emergence of ideas or a modified point of view.

The materials attempt to encourage this type of collaborative interaction. Teachers should also try to promote it through appropriate pre-activity instructions and post-activity feedback.

This type of interaction should also provide students with practice in unplanned speaking, building up their confidence in producing language in real time.

Initially the seminar discussions will be scaffolded, leading on later to each student leading their own seminar discussion, on a topic of their choice.

Presentation skills

The materials provide practice in giving formal presentations, gradually building up these skills through a variety of tasks (e.g., summarizing a text). Students are provided with opportunities to plan and rehearse their output. There is an early emphasis on delivering a presentation clearly, through good pronunciation, as many students neglect this area of presentation skills. This can lead to poor levels of comprehensibility in otherwise well-planned presentations. Teachers need to reinforce this emphasis on delivering a presentation in an audience-friendly way.

Language focus

The provision of planning time and opportunities for rehearsal should, in themselves, help to develop the accuracy, fluency and complexity of a student's language. However, students also need new language input in the form of functional exponents, sentence stems and other 'chunks' which may be common in academic speaking.

Relevant language items are presented within contextualized spoken mini-texts. The accompanying recordings allow a focus on pronunciation.

It is hoped that an explicit focus on certain language items and the provision of some form of restricted practice, will lead to greater uptake by the learners. This may not be immediate, but students are more likely to notice these target language items in subsequent exposure. This, in turn, may increase the chance of the language being added to existing resources.

Reflective learning

Early on in the course, students assess their own needs in relation to the target situation, by reflecting on their experience of different oral communication tasks (i.e., seminars, presentations, tutorials). They also assess their own strengths and weaknesses in the different micro-skills of speaking. Students revisit this self-assessment at the end of the course to measure their progress.

Students are also asked to engage in self-reflection and assessment through learner diaries, as well as through reviewing their own performance in seminars and presentations. These should help students to internalize the criteria necessary to evaluate their own performances, and so allow them to continue to develop after they have finished the course.

Unit summaries

These also provide an opportunity for the students to reflect on what they have done at the end of each unit. You may wish the students to complete the unit summaries in class or in their own time. If they complete them out of class, make sure you find time to discuss what the students have done.

Other features

Glossary: This contains a useful list of terms that the students will need to know during the course.

Study tips: These contain additional information that can be used by the students as a ready reference to a range of study issues related to the speaking skill.

Web resources: There are suggested web resources at the end of each unit. These also provide further areas of practice or study on topics or skills related to the unit.

Feedback

Peer feedback is promoted through the assessment of presentations and/or discussion review tasks which accompany each unit. These gradually become more extensive, as different criteria are added, depending on the focus of a particular unit. The same forms are reproduced for teacher feedback, (and can be photocopied), although it is expected that teachers will also comment on language performance. Note that all the photocopiable materials in this book are also available as downloadable files in the teacher's section of the EAS website – www.englishforacademicstudy.com.

Critical thinking

The topics and materials have been chosen in order to promote the thinking skills required in academic study. The spoken language materials reinforce the areas covered in the *EAS Writing* and *Extended Writing & Research Skills* books in this series, such as developing a point of view, analyzing issues from different perspectives and reaching a balanced conclusion.

Reading into speaking

Written texts are exploited in different ways in the materials. They are used as the basis for a straightforward exchange of information. They are also used as a basis for presentations, a stimulus for discussion and a source of support for a point of view. As above, learners are encouraged to bring a critical perspective to texts and articulate this where possible.

Scaffolded learning

The earlier units (1–5) provide more support in terms of language and skills work. The later units are more demanding. Unit 6 is a consolidation unit, which prepares students to lead a seminar, requiring them to put into practice the micro-skills which have been covered in previous units. The later units also expect students to carry out presentation and discussion tasks more autonomously.

Flexibility in the use of the materials

These materials have been organized so that there is a gradual progression of skills areas and different aspects of language use.

The core course is contained in Units 1–5. These develop the fundamental aspects of presentation and seminar discussion skills. Some of the information is highlighted under the headings **Presentation skills** and **Seminar skills**, which students can use for revision purposes. In addition, there are boxed **Study tips** containing ready reference of useful comments about a range of academic study issues.

Unit 6 is a consolidation unit, and focuses on student input, i.e., student-led seminars based on topics that students have chosen themselves. You may want to introduce this unit earlier in the course, and get students started on these seminars parallel to working through units 1–5.

Units 7–9 provide further opportunities to develop presentation skills as well as covering other useful aspects of the speaking skill, such as turn-taking (Unit 7), conducting a questionnaire and presenting a research proposal (Unit 9). Unit 10 is a second consolidation unit, providing students with an opportunity to reflect on what they have been learning.

Each unit contains a *Useful language* section and it is important to ensure that students actively attempt to use this language in their discussion and in giving presentations. The *Useful language* expressions are available in photocopiable form in Appendix 1. You can refer to this appendix for suggestions on ways to encourage use of these expressions.

It is estimated that each unit will take about two weeks to cover, based on three hours of input per week; this assumes considerable preparation on the part of the students. If the student seminars are introduced earlier than Unit 6, the core units will take longer. Students may also be giving individual presentations during the course, which will also affect the rate of progress through the materials. The ten units can provide material for between 60 and 80 hours, depending on student ability and input, and could form part of an intensive three week-course or a non-intensive twenty-week course.

There is considerable flexibility in the way the units can be exploited. Some listening and reading texts used to stimulate discussion are more challenging. You may wish to omit particular texts with some groups, or even particular units. If you omit any of the core units, you should ensure that the skills and language in these units are covered in an alternative way. With higher-level groups, you may want to introduce the ideas of a debate early on (see Unit 8).

All of the units have warm-up activities to get students thinking about the topic. However, you may find that some of these activities are not useful for your particular group, or you may come up with alternative activities.

Suggested route for 16-week course

Week	Contact hours	Unit
1	3	Unit 1
2	3	Unit 1
3	3	Unit 2
4	3	Unit 2 (introduce Unit 6)
5	3	Unit 3
6	3	Unit 3
7	3	Unit 4
8	3	Unit 4
9	3	Unit 5
10	3	Unit 5
11	3	Unit 7
12	3	Unit 7
13	3	Unit 8
14	3	Unit 8
15	3	Unit 9
16	3	Unit 10

Suggested route for 10-week course

Week	Contact hours	Unit
1	3	Unit 1
2	3	Unit 1
3	3	Unit 2
4	3	Unit 2 (introduce Unit 6)
5	3	Unit 3
6	3	Unit 3
7	3	Unit 4
8	3	Unit 4
9	3	Unit 5
10	3	Unit 5

Suggested route for 8-week course

Week	Contact hours	Unit
1	3	Unit 1
2	3	Unit 1
3	3	Unit 2
4	3	Unit 2 (introduce Unit 6)
5	3	Unit 3
6	3	Unit 3
7	3	Unit 4
8	3	Unit 5

Suggested route for 5-week course

Week	Contact hours	Unit
1	3	Unit 1
2	3	Unit 2
3	3	Unit 3
4	3	Unit 4
5	3	Unit 5

Note: This route would require the students to do most of the work themselves in advance of the lesson, including the listening activities. Teachers could then use the lesson for clarification and discussion.

Communicating in academic situations
Being a successful student

In this unit students will:
- reflect on their experience of speaking in an academic context;
- analyze their strengths and weaknesses in speaking;
- identify and practise language for agreeing and disagreeing;
- consider aspects of a successful presentation;
- give a short informal mini-presentation.

The topic of this unit concerns factors which may lead to improved academic performance among students. It is based on three major research projects carried out in the United States.

Introduction to the course

This is the first unit of the course, and the class dynamics are very important. You may wish to do an initial activity for both you and the students to learn each other's names as well as to create an atmosphere in which students feel secure and can participate fully.

You should begin with a brief introduction to the course, explaining that the main purpose of a 'speaking' course is to help students develop their speaking skills by actually speaking, through engaging in various tasks and participating in discussion. Developing presentation skills and seminar discussion skills are core strands which run throughout the course. Explain that these may be a challenge if students are nervous, but that confidence grows with practice. The initial tasks are designed to look at some of the activities students will be expected to engage in.

Task 1: Your experience of speaking English

1.1 Students will be anxious to know about the course and what is expected of them. The first task helps to set the context, as it shows students what will be expected on their future courses. This list has been drawn up on the basis of contacts with departments at the University of Reading, as well as from speaking to pre-sessional students once they have begun their course.

1.2 Encourage students to develop what they say, i.e., not simply say *yes* or *no*, but to talk about their experience in more detail, as prompted by the materials, e.g., what kinds of topics they presented on or the kinds of discussions they had.

1.3 Keep this activity brief; it is a way of concluding the discussion.

Task 2: Your attitude to speaking English

2.1 The aim of this task is to raise awareness of students' attitudes to speaking English.

2.2 Again encourage them to develop their ideas by giving reasons for their beliefs.

    a) Concerning the issue of speaking with a native-speaker accent, you might want to point out that this is not necessary, e.g., comprehensibility is important, but individual accent is perfectly acceptable and indeed often very attractive.

    c) Some students feel that they can be more direct in English, whereas others feel that lack of vocabulary and structure, or even the nature of the language itself, may inhibit them from fully expressing their personality.

2.3 ⊕ .1 You might play the recording once or twice depending on the level of your group.

Answers:
The students refer to points a, d, f and g.

2.4 You could do a chain drill around the class, keeping it short and lively, giving everyone the opportunity to say one or two expressions.

Answers:
(Stressed syllables are marked with ')
dis'cussion
contro'versial
disa'greement
pro'voke

2.5 Depending on your particular group, you might want begin with some controlled practice of the *useful language*.

It is important that students get into the habit of trying to use the language expressions regularly throughout the course; it is only through this kind of deliberate practice that these expressions will become part of their vocabulary.

Task 3: Agreeing and disagreeing

3.1 Students could briefly compare their responses to each statement.

3.2/3.3 ⊕ 2 A gapped transcript is provided in Appendix 2a if you wish to exploit this. You could photocopy that and have students fill in the gaps on it, rather than on the table provided in the Course Book.

Answers:

	Opinion	Useful language
a	agree	Absolutely. I totally agree.
b	partly agree	Yes, that's true, but …
c	disagree	I'm not sure I agree with you there. *
d	partly agree	I agree up to a point, but …
e	disagree	Not necessarily. **
f	agree	That's a very good point.

* You can point out that the disagreement is softened in this example, but it amounts to saying 'I don't agree'.
** This might need glossing as 'That is not always true'.

One of the key aspects of the course is that of getting students to use appropriate language exponents in their discussions. A highly controlled way of doing this would be to use the transcript.

Focus on the pronunciation of the target phrases. First, select a pair to 'perform' the first exchange to the class. Then highlight and drill the target phrase around the class, focusing on stress, intonation and fluidity. Repeat for the other exchanges, before letting students practise in pairs. Monitor for pronunciation of the target language.

After initially working with the text, encourage students to practise the exchanges without looking at the transcript, as this will mean they have to really think about what they are saying and how they say it.

1

3.4 This provides an alternative, less controlled practice than the one described in Ex 3.3, as students are asked to respond with any of the *useful language* phrases which coincide with their opinions and to provide support, rather than simply reading the transcript.

Another less controlled alternative is to provide prompts on the whiteboard (e.g., *a) succeed at university … manage your time*) to help students recall the content of the statements and get them to practise responding to each other, again using any of the *useful language* phrases, plus their own supporting opinions. Alternatively, provide new statements on the area of study skills for students to respond to.

The way you choose to practise the language will partly depend on the level of your class.

Task 4: Study skills for success

4.1 ⊙ 3 Get students to look at the list of points first, related to study skills, and ensure that they understand the meanings.

Answers:
a __4__ Plan ahead and begin working early.
b __6__ Choose areas to study that you are interested in.
c __1__ Find out what is important on your reading list.
d __5__ Ask a peer to read your work before submitting it.
e __2__ Use reading strategies to help you read quickly.
f __3__ Deal with stress by finding time for relaxation.

You may wish to exploit the recording/transcript further. Students may want to listen to/read certain sections again for detail they missed first time around. There are some useful details that are worth focusing on, such as asking tutors for advice on which books to read. Some of these areas are revisited in Unit 10, where two students are interviewed.

4.2 For the follow-up activity, you may need to elicit from students some of the skills they think are needed to activate the schema. For example, *Successful students need to:*
• *balance work and play;*
• *ensure that they plan their work according to a timetable;*
• *plan ahead and begin working well in advance of deadlines.*

Task 5: Prioritizing study skills

You could do this as a mini-pyramid discussion. First, students prioritize five points in pairs. They then join with another pair or regroup into threes and negotiate five points from the combined lists. The points individuals choose will depend on their own particular learning strategies. The teacher monitors to ensure the discussion moves forward.

Task 6: Tips for successful study – a mini presentation

Each group should have finalized their top five study skills as pieces of advice for new students.

6.1 Students should be in pairs or threes/fours. At this stage, discourage students from deciding who in the group will actually deliver the presentation (see Ex 6.3). This should ensure that they all remain fully involved, rather than handing over the initiative to the group presenter/s.

The presentation can take the form of either a poster or an OHT. Encourage students to be resourceful with poster design; remind them that the visual aspect is very important and they may in fact prefer to represent ideas through pictures rather than words.

a) Students may have a tendency to write too much; as you monitor groups, emphasize that only key words are important; too much information on an OHT detracts from its impact.

b) 🎧 4 Students listen to a model before they themselves need to give a presentation.

c) Again, the focus on language is to encourage students to try and make some of these expressions part of their vocabulary. Emphasize that these are expressions which will be useful time after time.

Refer students to Course Book Appendix 1, which provides further useful signpost language for presentations.

6.2 Go through the list of criteria for evaluating the delivery of a presentation, explaining the terms. Throughout the book, various aspects of presentations are worked on. 'Delivery' is the first aspect, and it is important that you emphasize the development of presentation skills throughout the materials.

6.3 Let them decide whether to choose one of their group to do the whole presentation or divide up the points so that everyone has an opportunity to speak. The practice allows for a rehearsal before 'going public'.

Note: All students in the group should participate in giving presentations at some stage during the course, but giving them the autonomy to decide who presents first allows more confident students to come forward and gives less confident students time to get used to the idea, see how it is done and have models.

6.4 Remind students of the important aspects of delivery of a presentation you discussed in Ex 6.2. Explain that they are going to evaluate each other on these criteria.

You will need to photocopy the assessment form that appears at the end of this unit for students (Handout 1). This form can also be used by you to give feedback on the presentations. The 'Other comments' section allows you to provide more detailed feedback on pronunciation or other language problems if you wish. If students do a joint or group presentation, they should still receive individualized assessment forms from both peers and teacher.

Note: An alternative assessment form in the form of a grid is provided in Appendix 2b, if you feel this would be more accessible for students. Whichever form you use, ensure students understand the different criteria.

Monitor this and encourage constructive criticism.

6.5 a) At the end of all the presentations, students should hand over the feedback forms to the presenters. Alternatively, you could collect them all in and redistribute them to the relevant people. Students should stay in their original presentation groups to 'digest' the feedback from their peers. Use this as an opportunity to make some general comments on what students can focus on next time in terms of improving their presentation skills.

b) Encourage students to give reasons for their views. Summarize with general comments on what students need to focus on overall.

Suggestions for presentations:
You might like to consider the following options:

- Choose strong students to present for each group, as good models for the whole class.

- Set up the first one or two presentations as a 'standardization', in which all students complete an evaluation form and discuss their responses in groups, before the teacher offers some constructive guidance on the performance. Obviously, you should choose stronger, more confident students for this.

- Spread presentations over several sessions instead of doing them all in one class.

Task 7: A successful presentation

7.1 This exercise gets students to think about various aspects of PowerPoint presentations. Encourage them to give reasons for their answers.

Answers:

	Presentation skill	Appropriate	It depends	Inappropriate
a*	The presenter puts as much information as possible on each slide.			✓
b*	The presenter uses colour and sound to liven up his/her slides.		✓	
c	The presenter reads from a script.			✓
d	The presenter memorizes a script and recites it.			✓
e	The presenter uses notes.	✓		
f	The presenter pauses after each main point.	✓		
g	The presenter reads all the information on the slide.			✓
h	The presenter stands in one place all the time.		✓	
i	The presenter speaks at the same speed all the time.			✓

* The assumption is that many students will use presentation software such as PowerPoint

Notes:
Point d: Memorizing a script can be a necessary prop for some students early on, but it should be emphasized that during the course they should try to move away from this towards the use of notes.

Point e: A useful technique with presentation software is for the presenter to print out a copy of the slides and make their notes on this, for reference during the presentation.

Point h: If the presenter is standing in a position that blocks the audience view of the screen, then obviously this is poor.

Point i: Using pace and emphasis effectively in a presentation is an important skill, for example, slowing down when giving important or complex information.

7.2 Monitor the discussion, and then get group views in plenary.

If you have video clips of presentations, show these and let students evaluate/discuss these recordings in the light of the presentation skills highlighted in Tasks 6 and 7 of this unit.

Task 8: Review

8.1 Research into language learning has shown that reflecting on the process of learning has a strong impact on the effectiveness of how you learn. One way of doing this is through keeping a diary, something students might initially be unsure about. The self-assessment form, which they could complete for homework, gives them some ideas on how to get started, with some concrete ideas they might potentially write about in their first entry. In a subsequent lesson they could go through their responses to this questionnaire in pairs or small groups.

8.2 Make sure you provide the students with the appropriate encouragement to complete the learner diary on a regular basis.

Note: At this stage, you might like to schedule individual presentations. These are really to give students confidence in performing before an audience and a chance to focus at an early stage on delivering a presentation clearly. Encourage them to choose their own topic.

Provide individualized feedback. You can use the form provided in Appendix 2c or devise your own. This may depend on the level of your group in terms of language and level of study.

Direct students to Course Book Appendix 4, which provides advice on preparing for a presentation.

Unit summary

You may want the students to complete the unit summaries in class or in their own time. If they complete them out of class, make sure you get some feedback during class time.

You may wish to set up some of the activities, either to clarify what to do, or to help get students thinking about the topics.

Some of the items can be done individually and others are best done in pairs or groups. When working outside the classroom, encourage students to find the time to meet with others and complete any pair or group activities.

1 This activity might need a bit of class discussion to prompt the students' thoughts on the subject.

2 If the students do this activity outside the classroom, you may wish to provide an incentive to meet and discuss; for example, you could set up the groups beforehand and specify that.

Web resources

The web resources provide further areas of practice or study on topics or skills related to the unit. These might change from time to time, but at the time of print they were as follows.

BBC Learning English: Better Speaking
A discussion programme that provides tips on how to become a fluent, confident speaker of English. Students can also hear learners of English from around the world talking about their speaking problems.
http://www.bbc.co.uk/worldservice/learningenglish/webcast/tae_betterspeaking_archive.shtml

BBC Learn English: Talking Business
A list of signpost language for presentations.
http://www.bbc.co.uk/worldservice/learningenglish/business/talkingbusiness/unit3presentations/expert.shtml

Ten top tips for successful study at university
Study tips for new students on the University of Reading website. It also has useful links to other study advice sections of the website.
http://www.reading.ac.uk/internal/studyadvice/sta-home.asp

Handout 1

Presentation assessment (Course Book Appendix 9a)

Name of presenter	
Pronunciation of sounds/words	not clear reasonably clear clear very clear
Intonation	not varied quite varied varied
Volume	too quiet appropriate
Speed	too fast too slow appropriate
Eye contact	none too little reasonable good very good

Other comments

Photocopiable

2 Seminars and discussions
Learning online

In this unit students will:
- identify characteristics of successful participation in discussions and seminars;
- consider problematic issues from different perspectives;
- practise summarizing the outcome of a discussion;
- examine the role of a chairperson in a discussion.

In this unit students are encouraged to look at various approaches to participating in a seminar discussion. Some nationalities at times find it very challenging to voice their opinions and take turns in this environment, so this unit looks at some of the micro-skills involved in successful participation in a discussion. This unit also encourages students to think beyond their own personal point of view.

Task 1: A successful participant in group discussions

1.1 The purpose of this exercise is to get students to look at their own role in a discussion and identify what they need to do more of. Some of the points could fit into either category.

Key:

	The participant ...	Good	It depends	Poor
a	listens to what others say and builds on this, adding his/her opinion.	✓		
b	tries to get other people to change their mind, and agree with his/her opinion.		✓	
c	always agrees with other people's opinions.			✓
d	does not say anything at all.			✓
e	explains his/her point in great detail, and at length.			✓
f	explains his/her points briefly.	✓		
g	is nervous about speaking, but makes himself/herself do it.	✓		
h	encourages others to speak, inviting them into the discussion.	✓		
i	only speaks when asked.			✓
j	asks other students to clarify what they mean, or to explain further.	✓		
k	changes his/her opinion during the discussion.		✓	

1.2 Monitor pairs during this discussion and ask some of them to share their ideas in plenary afterwards.

1.3 This encourages students to think about cross-cultural differences.

Task 2: Different perspectives on an issue

2.1 This exercise is designed to encourage students to think about one topic from a range of perspectives, going beyond a black-and-white view of the situation. Some interesting cultural elements might emerge, depending on how important the role of the school/teacher is seen to be. Make sure students understand the idea of perspectives.

Answers:
Example answers:

Teacher:	might consider other children in the class and how they are losing out because s/he cannot teach effectively
Parents:	might feel teacher is not challenging child, or be biased about child's behaviour
Headteacher:	might be concerned about school reputation
Child psychologist:	might consider it a challenge, and want to keep child in school to get to the root of the problem

2.2 Draw students' attention to the *useful language* for comparing perspectives.

2.3 🔊 5 Having already thought about the topic, students should be tuned in to the content of the recording.

Answers:
See transcript on page 64 (Course Book page 92) for answers.

Task 3: Reaching a balanced conclusion

3.1/3.2 In this exercise, as in Task 2, encourage lateral thinking. To scaffold the exercise more, you might wish to ask students initially to identify the key figures in each situation. As you monitor their discussions, remind students to think of the long-term consequences as well as the more immediate ones.
For example:
Statement 1:
- current school situation, where students may be running riot (short-term)
- general levels of respect in society dropping (long-term)

3.3 Emphasize that students should try and objectively discuss what the views of the different people involved might be, before giving their personal view.

Note: Task 4 focuses on language for summarizing a discussion, at the end of which students are asked to summarize their discussions from Task 3. You may wish to omit this. If you don't intend to cover Task 4 in the course, ask groups to summarize their discussion of each statement at this stage.

Task 4: Summarizing the outcome of a discussion

4.1 🔊 6 **Answers:**
The group agreed.

4.2 🔊 6 **Answers:**
1   we finally all agreed that
2   It's true that
3   this action should only be taken if

4.3 **Answers:**
(Stressed words are underlined)
we <u>finally</u> <u>all</u> <u>agreed</u> that … (3)
It's <u>true</u> that … (1)
<u>this</u> <u>action</u> should <u>only</u> be <u>taken</u> if … (4)

4.4 **a)** The three phrases in Ex 4.3 are reproduced in the *useful language* box. You can use these to clarify the significance of the bracketed numbers given for each phrase in the box (= the number of stressed words). Students could predict the stressed words in pairs, before a whole-class check with the teacher. You may like to drill some of these expressions with the group, with the focus on stress.

Answers:
(Stressed words are underlined)
After <u>much</u> <u>consideration</u>, we <u>decided</u> that … (3)
<u>All</u> <u>things</u> <u>considered</u>, we <u>felt</u> that … (4)
On <u>balance</u>, we <u>felt</u> that … (2)
We <u>couldn't</u> reach <u>agreement</u> on this <u>issue</u> … (3)
<u>Some</u> of us <u>felt</u> that … <u>whilst</u> <u>others</u> … (4)
We <u>recognized</u> that … (1)
We're <u>fully</u> <u>aware</u> that … (2)
One <u>has</u> to <u>acknowledge</u> that … (2)
<u>So</u>, <u>although</u> we <u>agreed</u> with the <u>statement</u>, we <u>stressed</u> that … (5)

Note: If there was no pause between *so* and *although*, then *so* would not be stressed. The comma indicates a 'spoken' pause.

You can highlight that the above stress patterns are 'neutral'. The speaker can shift the stress for contrastive purposes. For example, *On balance we <u>felt</u> that …* versus *On balance <u>we</u> felt that …*

b) 🔊 7 When students listen to the recording, they could follow the transcript and mark the stress in the appropriate place for consolidation. Alternatively, students could cover the transcript with   a piece of paper, listen to the first contextualized example 'unseen', repeat the target phrase from memory, then uncover the transcript and mark the stressed words. Repeat for the other examples.

c) Assign different statements to different groups. Encourage students not to script their summaries, but to rehearse them in their groups, incorporating the language from the *useful language* box.

4.5 Any comments or questions students have for the summarizing group should be about the content of their summary, rather than feedback on their performance.

Task 5: Online learning

5.1 **a)** In this task students should put into practice the skills they have been working on in the scaffolded tasks so far. Ask who has had experience of online learning. You might like to ask some specific questions to get them going.

Examples:
Have you ever studied online?
Is online learning popular in your country?
Is it possible to study your subject online?
What are the main differences between learning online and learning face-to-face?

b) The reading texts will give students some ideas to add to their own. You might want to give them the readings as homework.

5.2/5.3 For the discussion, divide the class into groups of five or six and appoint a chairperson for each group. Choose individuals you feel will be comfortable in the role and will keep things going.

Go over the list of responsibilities of the chairperson with everyone, as at some stage each individual will take that role. If you have a more reticent class, you could structure this activity more by setting it up as a formal debate in groups. One half of each group supports the motion; the other opposes it. You could also change the debate motion to: *Online learning is better than face-to-face learning*.

5.4 After students have filled in the appropriate form (Course Book Appendix 9b) and have fed back in pairs or small groups, round off with your own comments.

Give feedback to the class as a whole on the discussion. Pick up on points like group dynamics and interaction. Encourage proactive participation if students were passively waiting to be nominated during the seminars.

5.5 Again, you should briefly discuss with students what they might write about for this diary entry. If students have time and access to equipment, they might wish to take up the suggestion of recording their diary entries.

For a rationale, see:
Ho, Y. (2003). Audiotaped dialogue journals; an alternative form of speaking practice. *ELTJ*. 57(3), 269–277.

Unit summary

1 If the students discuss this outside the class, you may wish to start with a brief class discussion to raise interest in the topic.

2 **Answers:**
dominate, overview, participate, dominate, contribution, clarify, time, sum up

Web resources

mySkills: Academic skills at Essex: Seminar skills
This site gives detailed information about seminars in UK universities and has tasks to encourage students to think about how seminars are different to lectures and familiarize them with useful language.
http://www.essex.ac.uk/myskills/skills/seminars/seminarSkills.asp#04

Effective vision: thinking techniques
An article that looks at different approaches and activities that help students to see problems and issues from different perspectives.
http://www.effectivevision.co.uk/EVAHIThinkingTechiques1.pdf

Hong Kong Polytechnic University: English for academic purposes
Students can go to the *Brainstorming* section to find useful language for discussing ideas.
http://elc.polyu.edu.hk/cill/eap/

Examining underlying assumptions
Changing roles in the family

In this unit students will:
● develop awareness of how to help their audience follow a presentation;
● present an article to the class, using the language of presentations;
● consider the importance of anticipating arguments before a discussion;
● practise presenting opinions and counter-arguments in a discussion.

Overall, the purpose of this unit is to give students practice in identifying main points and being able to summarize them, a key skill in delivering effective presentations. They are also given further practice in seminar skills, through presentation of opinions and counter-arguments.

Task 1: The meaning of *family*

1.1/1.2 The aim of this task is to get students to question the assumptions they make about simple concepts, and examine how an interpretation of these concepts varies according to context.

Task 2: Aspects of family life

2.1/2.2 The questions here reflect some of the content of the articles which the students are asked to summarize later in this unit. These activities are designed to help to make the articles and subsequent presentations, which are based on the texts, more accessible to the class.

Task 3: Presenting an article (1)

This is a model for the following stage, where students have to present a text.

3.1 You may want to assign this reading task for homework.

3.2 This exercise focuses simply on producing an audience-friendly visual aid without too much detail. OHT 1 gives too much detail and is poorly laid out, making it difficult to distinguish between main and supporting points. Sections of the article are simply copied onto the OHT. OHT 2 is a good example, as it limits the amount of information and uses bullet points for clarity.

Answers:
A good visual aid:
● limits the amount of detail;
● is clearly laid out;
● does not distract the audience with too many 'effects' (sound, etc.).

3.3 🎧 8 This is a straightforward sequential summary. A longer article may require a more sophisticated summary of the main points.

3.4 Students should be able to identify the final extract of the text as the part where the presenter gives his own comments on the article.

3.5 🎧 9 You should point out the importance of this type of variety, particularly the need to slow down, pause and use stress to highlight key or complex information and allow the audience time to absorb it.

Answers:
See after Ex 3.6.

3.6 The students need to extract the useful language from the context of the transcript.

Answers:
Answers to Ex 3.5: stressed phrases are underlined; slowed down phrases are in square brackets.
Answers to Ex 3.6 are **in bold**.

As the title suggests, **this article deals with** an apparent change in the role men would like to play in family life. First of all, **it provides** some statistics to support this claim, then looks at two issues related to it: the decline in the social stigma attached to being a stay-at-home dad and the question of the resources needed to support men who choose this new role.

So, **the article reports that** increasing numbers of men would prefer to stop working or work less in order to look after their children and home. **It refers to** statistics from the government, which show that 200,000 men now stay at home full-time to look after their children.

The article also gives statistics from a magazine survey of 2,000 couples. As you can see, only <u>one-third</u> of those asked, <u>34 per cent</u> in fact, wanted to continue working full-time after having children. The <u>majority</u> either wanted to return to part-time work or become full-time househusbands. This is what the men in the poll said they wanted. **According to the article**, however, what stops them from actually giving up work and staying at home is, not surprisingly, money or worries about money.

The article then goes on to say that the social stigma attached to men stopping work to bring up a family is disappearing [… social stigma – this means something people might be ashamed of doing, that society would not approve of]. As I said, this is disappearing, so you now see more men coming to schools and playgroups to collect their children.

Finally, **the article argues that** more resources are needed to support these new full-time fathers, such as this website www.homedad.org.uk. **It quotes** a founder of the website as saying that most current resources for parents are aimed at mothers. So, **the article reports on** some interesting changes in social attitudes to work and fatherhood. However, **it doesn't mention** the effect of <u>socioeconomic</u> background on men's decisions or wishes regarding work and parenthood. I mean, the men who are choosing or wanting to give up work to become househusbands, [are these men from <u>high</u>, <u>middle</u> or <u>lower</u> income groups?] We don't know this from the text, but this could be significant data.

Task 4: Presenting an article (2)

4.1 Assign each pair/group of students one of the seven texts on pages 73–83 of the Course Book according to their interests and language abilities. The first three texts are more straightforward and would be more suitable for lower-level students.

4.2 You could give the reading texts out for students to read as homework. In the following class, they can prepare, practise and give the presentations, or the presentations can be spread over two classes.

Go through the *Presentation skills* guidelines. You can refer back to the *Househusbands* model to illustrate the points listed. You will need to monitor the preparation process to check they have understood the texts and are following the advice given in the *Presentation skills* guidelines.

4.3 Students will probably need guidance to ensure they are presenting the texts in an audience-friendly way.

Points to watch with the texts:

1   Encourage students to first identify headings for an OHT.
For example:
Text: *Family formation*
Possible headings:
- Births outside marriage
- Multiple births
- Age of women at childbirth
- Number of children per woman

2   Be careful that students signal to the audience when they are referring to 'quotations' or other types of secondary sources given within the texts. You could provide the necessary language for this (e.g., 'The article quotes one of the researchers …'). See the *Househusbands* text for examples.

3   *Affluent but anxious and alienated:*
Make sure students give the context by making it clear that the information is based on three studies, following people born in 1946, 1958 and 1970.

4   *Cradle of civilisation:*
This is quite long. You could tell students to read and present only as far as the paragraph which begins 'These findings are not good news for working parents …'.

4.4   **a)** Ensure you have enough copies of the form that appears at the end of this unit (Handout 2, Course Book Appendix 9c) for the class. Students have a copy in their books, but it is for reference purposes. The ones they fill in during class should be copies distributed by you, so they can be handed on to the presenters at the end. A teacher's feedback form is provided in Appendix 2d, with a space for other comments.

For each presentation, only <u>one</u> student per group should complete the form. If the presentation is a shared one, the group should complete one for each presenter if possible.

b) The other group members should 'pool' their comprehension after each presentation. Some international students form small study groups. They meet after lectures to try and help each other out with comprehension gaps. This stage is designed to promote this type of cooperation.

4.5   After the presentations have all been completed, you can exploit the texts further. You could put the titles on the board, with some key headings under each one, to remind students of the content. Alternatively, you could photocopy the OHTs for distribution around the class. These can form the basis of intercultural comparisons. Most of the texts are UK- or EU-specific. Obviously, students will not have statistics to hand from their own countries, but they might be able to speculate/comment on the trends and attitudes more generally.

Task 5: Arguments and counter-arguments

This section asks students to perform a task. It then introduces some useful language, before asking students to repeat a similar task, this time with a focus on trying to use some of the useful language.

5.1   The statements in this section relate to issues from the reading texts used, and revisit some of the areas from Task 1 of this unit.

5.2 Organize the students in groups of four and monitor the debate.

5.3 Round off with some feedback from the discussions, particularly any 'lively' ones that have occurred.

Did the students anticipate the arguments of their 'opponents' or were they taken by surprise?

5.4 🔊 **10 Answers:**
The expressions used in the recordings are:
Well, I think …
It seems to me that …
In my view, …
I take your point, but …
I understand what you're saying, but …
Well, I'm not sure if that's quite true …

5.5 Again you can take feedback from some of the pairs. Ask students which points within each discussion generated the most debate and 'conflict'.

Learner diary

Make sure the students are continuing to write their learner diaries.

Unit summary

1 **Answers:**
Pronunciation
Slow down when saying the <u>key</u> <u>words</u>
<u>Stress</u> particular words or phrases

Visual aids
Ensure key words are on your <u>slide</u>
Use <u>bullet</u> <u>points</u> and <u>headings</u> to ensure it is easy to read key points
Do not include too much <u>information</u> on each slide

2 Refer to Course Book page 25 for possible answers.

Web resources

Giving a successful presentation
This PowerPoint presentation reflects on presentation skills and common problems, and goes through the 'dos' and 'don'ts' of presentation-giving. It provides a good model of how to lay out presentation slides.
http://www.kent.ac.uk/uelt/learning/value/files/presentation08.ppt

Factbook on 'The family' by Po Bronson
This is a large, informally written collection of information and opinions about 'the family' from various sources such as news articles and US statistics. The information was collected together by an author when writing a book and gives an insight into American attitudes to families in the US and around the world. The information is divided into 'memos' or sets of notes on many different topics, including family roles, the future of the family, trends in childcare, etc.
http://www.pobronson.com/factbook/index.html

Handout 2

Presentation assessment (Course Book Appendix 9c)

Name of presenter		
Was the topic clearly identified at the beginning?	Yes	No
Were the main points of the article clearly explained?	Yes	No
Did the presenter give his/her own views on the article?	Yes	No
Did the presenter explain the meaning of any difficult or technical words?	Yes	No
Was the visual aid helpful?	Yes	No
Suggestions for improvement		

Reading into speaking
A healthy lifestyle

In this unit students will:
- use a text to support or modify their ideas;
- practise active listening;
- develop strategies to check their understanding as a listener;
- exchange information effectively by anticipating their listener's difficulties.

Task 1: Questionnaire

Students could interview each other with these questions.

You could ask students if there are any other questions they could add to the questionnaire, to determine whether they are leading a healthy lifestyle.

Task 2: Who is responsible?

Prompt students, if necessary, regarding who might share some responsibility for the issues in the two statements. These other 'parties' could be listed on the whiteboard at the end of the activity, as a round off and possible way in to Task 3. Focus on the differences of opinion and highlight the importance of academic debate.

Task 3: Preparation for a seminar discussion

3.1 Students are first asked to think about the topic and brainstorm some ideas before discussing with a partner. Encourage them to support their view with reasons.

At the note-making stage, encourage students to jot down who they think is responsible (the individual, the government, others?) and their main reasons.

3.2 Get students to read the article quickly to extract any points relevant to the discussion question. Set a time limit if necessary.

Elicit answers to the questions from some students.

3.3 A model mind map is provided, but students should try and develop their own notes. To encourage this, get students to look through the mind map and then close their books before completing their own notes.

3.4 Allow students quiet thinking time to plan and mentally rehearse what they want to say in the discussion. If you have a reticent class or groups within a class, you could appoint a chairperson to help give the discussions some structure and momentum. Refer students back to the chairperson's role and *useful language* from Unit 2.

3.5 There are plenty of summarizing slots during the course, in which students report back on their discussions. Make sure different students have an opportunity to practise this important skill.

Task 4: Being an active listener

4.1 This task asks students to reflect on their role as listeners and speakers in the discussion they have just had on obesity. It then provides some useful language for clarifying and confirming understanding and gives students controlled practice of this language. It asks students to have the discussion again, in different groups, this time with a focus on using the useful language and interactive strategies.

However, you may choose to do this section before the discussion on obesity in Task 3 and not ask students to redo the discussion.

4.2 🎧 11 Go over the *useful language* sections for clarifying and confirming understanding in preparation for the listening exercise.

Answers:
The expressions used in the recording are:
So what you're saying is …
So in your view, …
Do you understand what I mean?
I'm not sure I understand what you mean.

4.3 You might want to make a copy of the *useful language* phrases to cut up in strips and distribute to students to encourage their use.

4.4 If you feel that students would not want to redo the same topic, you can choose another health-related topic for students to discuss at this stage. The other topics in the unit may provide ideas (smoking, junk food, stress).

4.5 Students complete the form in Course Book Appendix 9d and share constructive feedback with other members of their group.

Task 5: Comparing information

5.1 This activity is a warm-up for further discussion on the topic on stress. Encourage students to think of their own experience.

5.2/5.3 Go through the instructions with the students before designating which article each student should read for homework (pages 85–86, or 87–88). With weaker students, before doing Ex 5.3 you might like those who have read the same article briefly to confer, to ensure they have the same key points.

The activity aims to make students more sensitive to their interlocutor and audience at the level of comprehensibility, in both discussions and presentations. Round off by re-emphasizing this point.

5.4 Make sure there is a genuine exchange of information, orally – do not let students read what the other has written, as this defeats the purpose.

Key:

	Article A: **Stress: To what extent can it be controlled?**	**Article B:** **Stress: Keeping things in perspective**
Definition of stress	Stress is essentially what individuals experience when they feel threatened or under pressure.	'Adverse reaction people have to excessive pressure or other types of demand placed on them.' A temporary feeling of being under pressure – not what you feel when under pressure but how you act.
Examples of symptoms of stress	A feeling of nervousness, accelerated heart rate, increase in rate of breathing, tension in the neck/shoulders, sick feeling in stomach, depression, headaches, fatigue.	Physical – tiredness, nausea, headaches, muscle tension, nervous twitches, altered sleep patterns. Behavioural – aggression, anxiety, poor decision-making, inability to prioritize, difficulty in concentrating, feelings of failure, mood changes, isolation.
Suggestions for dealing with stress	• meditation, physical activity (gym, aerobics), in touch with nature (gardening, walking), taking deep breaths • deal with causes of stress • change lifestyle	• talk to someone – family or friend • keep a diary • talk through your diary • learn how to relax – breathing • exercise regularly • plan breaks in your day

5.5 Encourage students to summarize their findings. Get students to reflect on how active their listening skills were.

5.6 This gets students thinking about how to transfer information – using sources for different purposes.

Learner diary

Make sure the students are continuing to keep their learner diaries up to date.

Unit summary

1 It is useful for students to reflect on these questions before discussing with others.

2 **Answers:**
So what you're <u>saying</u> is …
Am I <u>making</u> <u>sense</u>?
I don't quite <u>follow</u> <u>you</u>.
Could <u>you</u> <u>repeat</u> <u>that</u> <u>please</u> / Could <u>you</u> <u>explain</u> <u>that</u> <u>point</u>
Do you <u>follow</u> <u>what</u> <u>I'm</u> <u>saying?</u> / Do you understand what I mean?
If I <u>understand</u> <u>you</u> correctly …

Web resources

BBC Learning English: 6 minute English

Listening practice: A conversation on the topic of stress. There is also a glossary of words related to the topic.

http://www.bbc.co.uk/worldservice/learningenglish/radio/specials/1630_144_6min_backup/page30.shtml

Quizzes based on VOAs Special English Programmes

Topic-based grammar and vocabulary quizzes. Students can try the quizzes in the *Science Reports* section on health-based topics, such as 'Chocolate and the heart', 'Cholesterol in Young Men', 'Stop Smoking'.

http://www.manythings.org/voa/

5 The use of data
The influence of the media

In this unit students will:
- practise describing charts and data;
- practise seminar skills by building on what previous speakers have said;
- identify and practise using phrases to refer to other speakers.

Task 1: Matching definitions

The purpose of this task is to activate schemata about TV programmes and possibly to comment on the kinds of programmes popular on local television, e.g., soap operas which have been running for many years, as well as the more recently popular *Big Brother* or *Survivor* genre of programme.

Answers:
a)   soap opera – 2) A long-running drama of the day-to-day experiences of a community of characters.
b)   quiz show – 3) A programme in which contestants try to score points by answering questions correctly.
c)   reality TV – 9) A programme in which a group of people (usually from the public) are filmed over a period of time.
d)   chat show – 7) A programme in which a presenter asks a celebrity to talk about him/herself.
e)   sitcom – 10) A comedy of character and situation, involving the same characters in each episode.
f)   documentary – 4) An informative, in-depth examination of a fairly serious topic.
g)   phone-in – 1) A programme in which the public takes part by phoning in with comments.
h)   classic drama – 6) An adaptation of a major work of literature.
i)   makeover programme – 8) A team of experts redecorates your house, redesigns your garden or changes your image.
j)   game show – 5) A programme in which contestants take part in various games to win prizes.
k)   mini-series – 11) A programme which has several episodes, with the same characters.

Task 2: Discussion: TV programmes

2.1   This exercise should emerge naturally from the first one, as a follow-up discussion. Encourage students to think about why certain types of programmes are popular, e.g., why reality TV is so popular in recent years.

2.2   This should be a brief activity – limit each speaker to two minutes; the main point of interest is their opinion of the programme.

Presentation skills

You might like to choose this moment to get students to think about what they have already learned about presentation skills – a brief five-minute review of what has been covered so far.

Ask them in what way data could have a positive impact on a presentation.

Task 3: Presenting information

3.1 Give students time to familiarize themselves with the graph.

Answers:
Accept any reasonable alternatives.
People aged 15–24 are the most likely to go to the cinema.
The percentage of young people going to the cinema regularly has risen since 1984.

3.2 🔊 12 **Answers:**
The point being made is given in the final line (*cinema remains popular, despite videos, DVDs and computer games*).

3.3 🔊 12 **Answers:**
<u>This graph shows</u> monthly visits to the cinema by age groups between 1984 and 2003.

<u>As you can see</u>, young people aged between 15 and 24 are the most likely age group to go to the cinema. Fifty-four per cent of this age group attended the cinema once a month or more in Great Britain in 2003. In 2003, 39 per cent of children aged seven to 14 went to the cinema once a month or more, <u>as can be seen from this line here</u>. The percentage for both these age groups has risen noticeably since 1984.

<u>From this data, it is clear that</u> going to the cinema is still a popular form of entertainment, despite the arrival of videos, DVDs and computer games.

3.4 If you have weaker students in the class, you may like to have some graphs or charts available to distribute to them. However, as far as possible encourage students to find their own, as this is an opportunity for them to decide the content of the class, by choosing material that interests them.

Task 4: Listening

The purpose of this listening is to feed in ideas (an independent media, bias, propaganda) that are relevant to the discussion topics that follow in subsequent tasks. It is a stand-alone activity, however, that can be omitted, depending on the level of students, time available, etc.

4.1 🔊 13 Give students time to read the questions first and ensure they understand them. Then play the recording.

4.2 Let students work in pairs to check the answers in the transcript.

4.3 Encourage an open class discussion about this topic.

Task 5: Building on what the previous speaker has said

This might be a good opportunity for students to review what they have covered in the *seminar skills* tips. Ask them to look back over highlighted sections to remind themselves about the key factors in being an effective participant in a seminar or discussion.

One of the key skills in participation in seminars is building on what previous speakers have said. Very often students are keen to say what they want and may ignore what has been previously said. This is related to the point of being an active listener.

There is some flexibility in the order in which Tasks 5 and 6 are done. An alternative to using the order given in the book would be to do the following:

1   Students discuss one of the topics in Ex 6.1 in groups;
2   Work through Ex 5, which highlights the *useful language*;
3   Form different groups and redo the discussion topic from Ex 6.1 or choose one of the other topics, this time trying to use some of the *useful language*.

These are discussion points designed to preview the content of the listening activity.

5.3   🔊 14 You may have to play the recording twice.

Answers:
Suggested answers:
a) The man believes there should be limits on freedom of speech.
b) People can't be trusted to use the right of freedom of speech responsibly; rights should be limited in order to protect minorities from potentially dangerous remarks.
c) He doesn't change his opinion.

5.4/5.5   This asks students to extract the *useful language* from the context of the transcript.

Answers:

When you say … do you mean that … ?

As you said … You made an interesting point about …

following on from that point … regarding what you both say about … Can I also pick up on your point about …

those are fair arguments, but you make the point that …

As I said before …

Task 6: Group discussions: Referring to other opinions

6.1   Ensure that students understand the topics – you might like to give a few ideas for each one. Divide the class into groups of four or five. Make sure they do not spend too long choosing the topic.

6.2   Encourage the students to commit ideas to paper, in order to have something concrete to contribute to the discussion.

6.3   Monitor the discussions, giving encouragement where necessary.

6.4   Students complete the form in Course Book Appendix 9e. The purpose of this form is to encourage students to reflect on their performance, with a view to looking at how it can be improved.

Task 7: Over to you

You might like to let students know about this task at the beginning of the unit, so they have more time to look for material. Get students to choose articles which they think will be of interest to the class, to provoke discussion.

Learner diary

Encourage the students to continue to reflect on their progress.

Unit summary

1   **Answers:**
    a) It shows the changing pattern of people going to the cinema by age.
    b) In 1987, 88 per cent of young people aged between 7 and 14 went to the cinema, but in 1998, the figure had risen to 97 per cent. Similarly, in 1987, 74 per cent of 15–34 year olds went to the cinema, but in 1998 it was 96 per cent.
    c) The number of people aged 35+ going to the cinema also rose in the 1980s and 1990s, from 21 per cent to 60 per cent. Between the years 1996–2002, the number of cinema-goers aged between 7 and 34 was relatively stable. For the same age bracket, there was also a decrease in cinema-goers from 2002–2003.
    d) Individual response.
    e) Individual response.

2   **Answers:**
    a) *Can I pick **up on** John's point …*
    b) *Following **on** from that point …*
    c) *This article **makes** some fair arguments …*
    d) *This article makes **an** interesting point about …*

Web resources

UEFAP: Speaking in academic contexts: Mathematical and scientific symbols
A comprehensive list of numbers and symbols such as fractions, ordinal numbers, etc., and a guide to how they are pronounced in English. Students can go to the mathematical and scientific symbols page by clicking on *symbols*.
http://www.uefap.com/speaking/spkfram.htm

Hong Kong Polytechnic University: Describing trends (data)
This site provides definitions and example sentences using the language of trends, such as *rise, drop, increase, etc.* There is also a practice exercise.
http://elc.polyu.edu.hk/cill/exercises/trends.htm

6 Consolidation unit

In the past five units, students have worked on the following skills:
- presenting their point of view and looking at different perspectives;
- presenting, agreeing with and countering an argument;
- building on what previous speakers have said;
- taking the role of chairperson;
- using appropriate language phrases.

You will need to look at this unit out of sequence (i.e., at an earlier point in the course) if you intend to run student-led seminars in parallel with working through the earlier units of the book. You could look at it with students after Unit 3, for example, as students will have done some work on seminar skills by then.

The purpose of this unit is for students to put into practice the skills they have been working on developing in previous units. In the section on seminar skills and presentation skills, you should encourage them to review what they have done in the first five units. They should also review the *useful language* phrases.

1   If, in Unit 5, you did not revise *Seminar skills* and *Presentation skills* boxes from the first half of the book, elicit from students what they have learned so far in terms of improving:
   • their seminar and discussion skills;
   • their presentation skills.
   Then get them to look at the list of skills covered, given at the start of the unit.

2   You could elicit some ideas about topics from the group, stressing the need to choose controversial topics.

3   Ensure students know how a seminar works (they will already have practised aspects of this in the discussion in previous units).

4   The teacher should do the first seminar as a model. You could use one of the model presentations in Appendices 2e to 2h, depending on which you think would be of more interest to your group. Let students know the seminar topic in advance (i.e., in the lesson before) so they can think of ideas. It is very important that you present the ideas briefly, within three to four minutes, and then let them get on with the discussion, saying only as much as you need to in order to keep things going. You may need to nominate students to speak, choosing more forthcoming students in order to get the ball rolling.

After the discussion, sum up in brief. Then ask the students how successful they felt the discussion was, in terms of their participation. Emphasize the importance of individual participation as support for the leader of the discussion.

Tasks 1–4: Organizing the student-led seminars

Encourage students to choose their own topics. Remind them about Appendix 5, which contains a list of possible seminar topics, in case they have difficulties in choosing topics of their own. If they have difficulties in deciding on a topic, you could tell them they may have to do a compulsory one. **Make sure that the topics they choose are suitable for discussion, accessible and of interest to the group.**

You will need to do a list of names and topics, with specific dates. Students should know clearly when they need to lead the seminar. In the lesson before each scheduled seminar, remind the whole class of the topic for that seminar, so they have an opportunity to think of ideas to contribute. You might like to do a table like the one here.

Name	Topic	Date

If you are on a shorter course (less than ten weeks): you will need to look at this unit very early on, and organize students to conduct seminars throughout the course, so they run parallel with the materials being worked on.

If you have a larger class: you could remove some of the students and place them as observers outside the 'circle' and assign them observation tasks.

If time is limited: students could double up. In this case they would prepare the initial presentation together and present it jointly (e.g., one student presenting the points for, the other presenting the points against). The class would then divide into two groups seated apart, with the two seminar leaders leading separate discussions (running concurrently) on the same topic.

Make copies of the assessment form at the end of this unit (Handout 3, Course Book Appendix 9f) for participants or observers to use. A teacher's version is provided in Appendix 2i. An alternative teacher feedback form is also provided in Appendix 2j.

Learner diary

The consolidation unit would be a good time to review some of the issues raised in the learner diaries.

Web resources

Hong Kong Polytechnic University: Videos
Video clips of simulated example presentations including examples of <u>bad</u> presentation-giving. There are also video clips of a model seminar.
http://elc.polyu.edu.hk/EAP/Audio-visual/

UEFAP: Speaking in academic contexts: Presenting a seminar paper
A guide to how to structure a seminar presentation. It gives plenty of examples of useful language for introductions, referring to graphs, etc. Students can follow the link *Presentation* to *Presenting a seminar paper.*
http://www.uefap.com/speaking/spkfram.htm

Handout 3

Assessing seminar leader's role: Check list (Course Book Appendix 9f)

1	Was the seminar topic appropriate, for example, a topic of interest to the group, and one they could participate in?	Yes / No
	Please comment	

2	Did the seminar leader give enough information about the topic in the beginning?	Yes / No
	Please comment	

3	Did the leader manage the seminar successfully? For example: – keep the discussion going; – allow everyone the opportunity to speak; – ensure one individual did not dominate.	Yes / No
	Please comment	

4	In what way could the seminar discussion have been improved?
	Please comment

Photocopiable

7 Supporting your point of view
The world of work

In this unit students will:
- prepare for a discussion by thinking through the issues beforehand;
- use a listening source to support their viewpoint;
- consider strategies for entering into a discussion;
- research and plan a presentation.

The emphasis in this unit is on encouraging students to use a range of resources related to the topic of work, in order to give practice in discussing a number of controversial issues. Students should be encouraged to use the skills they have been developing in previous units, particularly in using resources to support their ideas.

Task 1: Your attitude to work

1.1 Discuss the first item *(The amount I earn)* with the class as a whole. Encourage discussion about what the amount of money earned represents, e.g., status, a big house. Get students to engage in a discussion about what their values are; if they say money is the main priority, tease out what this represents to them.

1.2 This questionnaire is actually used in career guidance, helping people find the career which suits them. The questionnaire helps people identify the key 'drivers' which motivate them, and encourages them in the pursuit of their goals.

The scoring system is slightly complex, so read the instructions carefully and complete sections 1 and 2 in class to ensure students understand it. There is an example worked out at the end of the unit, with scoring. Get students to fill in the remaining sections at home. In the next lesson, give them the photocopied 'key' (Appendix 2k) to analyze the results in class. You can then put them in groups to decide if they agree with the 'key drivers' which the analysis throws up. Finish this by getting each group to report back on their discussion.

This should be a light activity, one the students enjoy, and should not be taken too literally.

Example of analysis of a completed questionnaire:
In the worked-out example at the end of the unit, AF is the highest motivation factor, followed closely by CR and AU. Four of the drivers appear to have no influence at all as a motivating factor.

Task 2: Finding a job in your country

This task gets students to move from looking at work issues in general to looking more specifically at what is happening in their own countries. If there are enough nationalities in your group to divide them according to nationalities, then you could get them to first discuss the questions in relation to their own country, then compare in a whole-class discussion with the situation in other countries.

Task 3: Gender at work

The statistics in this table act as a stimulus to get students thinking about the issue of gender in the workplace. Encourage them to comment on the differences between 1975 and 2006, e.g., the number of women who work; the percentage of female managers and directors, the percentage of women who return to work after giving birth.

Encourage students to think about trends in their own countries.

Task 4: Equal opportunities

4.1 Ensure that students understand this topic. Encourage general discussion in relation to these questions, monitoring pairs, and asking for some comments in plenary.

4.2 Reading the paragraph helps set the interview in context; give students a few minutes to do this.

4.3/4.4 🎧 15 Give students a few minutes to read the questions and then play the recording of the interview.

4.5 Divide the class into small groups – you may want to appoint a chairperson or let the students do this.

Task 5: Taking your turn

The issue of being able to enter a discussion at a particular point to make a contribution is one that students find very challenging. Task 5 gets them to think about this.

Elicit responses from students. Get them to look at the *useful language* for taking turns and think about how they could have used it in Task 4. Tell them they need to try and use this language in the following discussions.

Task 6: The changing nature of work in the 21ˢᵗ century

This task gives students practice in planning a presentation.

6.1 Get students to work on this in pairs, using dictionaries if necessary. Then clarify the meanings of the words briefly in plenary.

6.2 Encourage groups to choose different topics and then let them work through the questions in order to help them develop a focus for this. You might like to suggest groupings rather than leave it up to individuals to form their own, in order to ensure there is a good balance of levels/skills.

Work through the example on teleworking with students first.

6.3 You could limit this stage to class feedback on the group discussions instead of asking students to extend these into full presentations.

6.4 If doing a presentation, students should prepare collaboratively. Set a schedule and time limits for the presentations. When students give their presentations, you may want to formalize the feedback with feedback sheets; or simply have an informal discussion about each presentation, based on the criteria here. Your choice will depend on your group.

Learner diary

At this stage you should check with students to ensure they are still finding keeping a diary a useful activity. If not, it is not necessary for them to complete it. You could let this be a personal decision.

Career Drivers Questionnaire

What are your drivers? How do they influence your career? Complete the questionnaire below to help you assess your own career drivers.

There are no right and wrong answers. You have a total of 50 points. Allocate ten points – no more, no less, between the nine items in each of the five sections. If you wish, you may allocate ten points to one item if the other items in the section are of no importance to you.

SECTION ONE

These things are important to me:

1. [ ] I seek a high standard of living.
2. [ ] I wish to influence others.
3. [4] I only feel satisfied if the output from my job has real value in itself.
4. [4] I want to be an expert in the things I do.
5. [2] I seek to be creative at work.
6. [ ] I strive to work only with people I like.
7. [ ] I choose jobs where I am 'my own boss'.
8. [ ] I take steps to be 100% financially secure.
9. [ ] I want to acquire a social status that other people will respect.

SECTION TWO

In my working life I want to:

10. [ ] become an expert in a chosen field.
11. [4] build close relationships with others at work.
12. [ ] become a leader in teams and organizations.
13. [ ] be part of 'the establishment'.
14. [2] take decisions that I really believe in.
15. [ ] get the highest paid jobs.
16. [ ] have a job with long-term security.
17. [4] take my own decisions about how I spend my time at work.
18. [ ] create things that people associate with me alone.

Source: © Garrat, B. & Frances, D. (1994) Managing Your Own Career. London: HarperCollins.

SECTION THREE

If I am considering a new career opportunity:

19. [ ] I am drawn to roles with high social status.
20. [2] I wish to be seen as a real specialist in my field.
21. [ ] I want to work to make a contribution to the wider community.
22. [ ] I want to look ahead at life and feel that I will always be okay.
23. [ ] I seek influence over others.
24. [ ] I wish to build warm personal relationships with people at work.
25. [ ] I want a high standard of living.
26. [5] I want a degree of control over my own job.
27. [3] Producing things that bear my name attracts me.

SECTION FOUR

I would be disappointed if:

28. [ ] my work was not part of my 'search for meaning' in life.
29. [ ] I did not practise highly skilled work.
30. [ ] I could not afford a high standard of living.
31. [6] my job gave no opportunity to create something new or different.
32. [ ] I did not know where I would stand on retirement day.
33. [4] I worked without friends.
34. [ ] I did not receive recognition or honours.
35. [ ] I had to refer to others for decisions.
36. [ ] I wasn't in charge of people.

SECTION FIVE

A 'good' job means to me:

37. [2] avoiding being a cog in a big wheel.
38. [ ] an excellent income.
39. [ ] plenty of time to study specialist subjects.
40. [ ] being a person who takes important decisions.
41. [ ] producing products or services that have my name on them.
42. [4] having good relationships with other people.
43. [ ] being 'in charge' of others.
44. [ ] being secure.
45. [4] doing what I believe is important.

Scoring the career drivers questionnaire

Copy your score for each question onto the answer grid below (Note: the numbers are *not* in sequence) and then add up the scores in each vertical column.

1	2	3 4	4 4	5 2	6	7	8	9
15	12	14 2	10	18	11 4	17 4	16	13
25	23	21	20 2	27 3	24	26 5	22	19
30	36	28	29	31 6	33 4	35	32	34
38	43	45 4	39	41	42 4	37 2	44	40

Now add the score in each vertical column and insert the totals below

		10	6	11	12	11		
MR	PI	ME	EX	CR	AF	AU	SE	ST

Source: Garrat, B. & Frances, D. (1994). *Managing Your Own Career*. London: HarperCollins.

Unit summary

1   By this stage, your students might be able to discuss this without any set-up.

2   These questions require student reflection. Encourage them to spend time thinking about these issues, particularly how to improve performance.

Web resources

Hong Kong Polytechnic University: Presentation planner
This presentation planner helps students to structure their presentations and provides a pro-forma for them to complete. They can then print it out as a script, notes on cards or a slide show and even listen to a native speaker giving the presentation using the Text-to-Speech Dialog Wizard.
http://elc.polyu.edu.hk/cill/tools/presplan.htm

BBC Learning English: Business English: Working Abroad
A sophisticated, interactive site that links with an English language radio programme. Students can listen to other students and experts discussing work and jobs abroad and also learn vocabulary, try quizzes and do exercises.
http://www.bbc.co.uk/worldservice/learningenglish/business/wab/

Collecting and presenting data
Protecting the environment

In this unit students will:
- design a questionnaire and obtain feedback on it;
- collect and present data;
- participate in a debate;
- give a presentation on a global issue.

Students have filled in questionnaires in Units 4 and 7. This is an opportunity for them to design their own questionnaire, analyze data and report to the class. The focus can be on group, rather than individual, presentations.

If it is not practical for students on your course to design, pilot and administer their own questionnaires out of class, then simply work through Ex 1.1–1.5, which can be done in class, and omit Ex 1.6 and Tasks 2–4, which look at the process from designing to administering your own questionnaire.

Because they depend on students meeting in groups to do out-of-class preparation that may require some time to complete, Tasks 2–4 need to be scheduled and spread over a series of lessons, while you continue to work through other material.

The best approach would be to set aside some class time in which to work through those parts which can be done in class, while setting deadlines for the completion of the out-of-class work (drafting the questionnaire prior to Task 2; revising the questionnaire in Ex 2.4; administering the questionnaire in Task 3; preparing the presentation in Task 4). Students will need to bring their completed group work to a subsequent class in order to move on to the next stage. Students need to be reminded that the success of each subsequent stage of the process depends on them collaborating effectively, completing the work and bringing copies to class when required.

Task 1: Designing a questionnaire

1.1 Do this task in class as a model before students choose the subject for their own questionnaire. Encourage students to think about the attitude to protecting the environment and recycling in their own countries. You may want to choose some ideas from the list here to stimulate students' ideas.

- *What do you recycle in the home?*
- *Is there a collection of recyclable goods in your area?*
- *Do you feel it is important to recycle goods?*
- *Do you switch off lights when you leave a room?*
- *How often do you take a bath?*
- *How often do you take a shower?*
- *Do you know how much energy you use every month?*
- *What do you do with newspapers/bottles and jars/plastics/old clothes?*
- *On short trips do you tend to walk or take the car?*
- *Do you think people should take fewer trips on planes in order to cut down on fuel emissions?*

1.2 **Answers:**
Possible answers:
Question 1: inappropriate question, as people often do not like to state their age, and culturally you do not ask in Western society. An alternative might be to have a multiple-choice question, with a range of ages, e.g., 18–25, 26–40, etc. Adding tick boxes would also make it easier to analyze and report results.

Question 2: how often is *often*? Again, a system of categories would get better results, e.g., *once a week* or *less than three times a week*, etc.

Question 3: this question is very vague – recycle what? More detail needed. It also assumes people recycle. There is no 'never' option.

Question 4: not a useful question; maybe they don't, or maybe they do but never buy them; and what exactly are environmentally friendly products? Give examples.

1.3 Monitor while students are preparing, giving guidance where necessary, especially getting them to think about any questions that might be poorly designed.

1.4 Try and ensure that students identify flaws in each others' questionnaires. You could take some of the better examples and ask students to read them or put them on the whiteboard.

1.5 This can be done as a mingle activity. Go through the *useful language* box to ensure that students know what *the respondents* and *the subjects* refer to.

1.6 You may want to have a hand in grouping the students in order to try and ensure each group has one student who has good IT skills.

Students prepare the first draft of the questionnaire out of class. Show them the following model of the layout.

- Title on top
- A short introduction to the purpose of the survey
- Personal information if necessary, e.g., sex/age range
- The survey questions
- A 'thank you' note at the end

Example:

> **A student budget**
>
> The purpose of this survey is to find out what students spend their money on each week. We would very much appreciate it if you could help by taking a few minutes to fill in this questionnaire.
>
> 1
> 2
> 3
> ...
>
> Thank you for your help.
> X and Y

Tell students that the personal information given at the beginning is important if they want to make comparisons between answers to different questions.

Example:
Women recycled products more frequently than men.
Fifty-six per cent of women recycled, whereas only 45 per cent of men recycled.

Task 2: Piloting your questionnaire

2.1-2.3 In this piloting stage it is important that students get feedback from their peers so they can see which questions work and which do not, either because the answers they yield are not clear or because they do not give the information which the designer of the questionnaire wants.

2.4 Encourage students to show you the final version of their questionnaire for correction before they make the copies for distribution.

Task 3: Administering your questionnaire

Suggest that students distribute the questionnaire to a range of people, not only students on the course.

Task 4: Reporting back on your findings

4.1 Discuss the advantages/disadvantages of the ways data can be presented. Encourage students to decide the best way for their particular findings.

You could ask stronger students to produce more complex findings by, for example, cross-referencing age and/or gender with answers to other questions.

4.2 🎧 16 **Answers:**
Most of the respondents claimed that …
Approximately a third of those interviewed …
Just over 50 per cent of the subjects …

4.3 Make sure students take the opportunity to practise language from Ex 1.5. If you wish, this activity could be extended by having students give a formal-style presentation. Allow ten minutes for each group, and two minutes for questions.

Task 5: Participating in a debate

This is an optional activity; students are unlikely to be required to participate in a debate in their future studies, but this is an alternative way of practising some of the skills they need for participation in a seminar.

5.1 This topic could be set up as a debate, a formal way of presenting ideas. Alternatively you could set it up as a seminar topic for discussion. In either case, remind students about the importance of looking at different perspectives.

You could also provide the class with another debate motion:
Protection of the environment is mainly the responsibility of governments of the developed world.

This will allow two teams (A and B) to debate the motion given in the Course Book, while the rest of the class acts as the audience and judges. The latter then form two teams (C and D) to debate the motion given here while the members of A and B act as audience and judges.

5.2/5.3 Timing can be decided according to the group you have, e.g., you might allow the speaker for each team three minutes and then allow the discussion to run for about 15 minutes. It is important that you set clear time restrictions for students.

5.4 You may want to let the other students 'vote' to decide which team was more convincing.

Task 6: Perspectives on global issues

6.1 Remind students of Unit 2, on Education, when they had to think of the short-term and long-term consequences. You might want to do one as an example (see below), working through Ex 6.1–6.3 and building up ideas on the board. Ensure students understand the concepts/vocabulary before they begin the task.

Example:

Problem	Consequences
The use of fossil fuels	– more pollution → environmental damage – oil will run out – more wars to control access to oil

6.2/6.3 **Example:**

Topic: The use of fossil fuels	
Possible solutions	**Evaluation of solution**
– use renewable resources	– investment needed – can only be used in certain conditions (solar, wind power)
– impose personal/national limits on carbon emissions (a carbon allowance)	– difficult to enforce – unfair on developing world

Conclusion:
Both solutions could be partially effective.
Immediate political agreement needed.
Investment/enforcement crucial.

6.4 Ensure that each group chooses a different problem, to avoid overlap at the presentation stage.

Unit summary

1   Answers:

Designing a questionnaire
- You should make sure you have a clear focus for your questionnaire.
- Your questions should be easy to understand and should elicit relevant information.
- Avoid questions that are unclear, irrelevant or don't elicit the information that you need.

Administering a questionnaire
- Collect data by interviewing people face-to-face, over the phone or by e-mail.
- Make sure your questions are clear by practising them with someone you know.

Presenting data that you have gathered
- Decide how to present your data, e.g., bar chart, graph, table, etc.
- Highlight significant data or trends.
- Discuss the implications of this data.
- Evaluate the design of the questionnaire.

2   These questions require student reflection. Encourage them to spend time thinking about these issues, particularly how to improve performance.

Answers:

a)   Answers depend on students

b)   Possible answers: good public speaking skills and ability to connect with one's audience; planning skills; critical thinking skills, e.g., the need to predict the other team's arguments; ability to explain or argue a point clearly and persuasively; ability to respond to counter-arguments assertively.

c)   They can improve your ability to plan and set out arguments in a clear structured way (in essays, etc.); they can improve your critical thinking, discussion and questioning skills (in seminars, etc.); they can help your listening skills (in lectures and seminars).

d)   Possible arguments for:
- Use of fossil fuels causes pollution and climate change: we need to change bad environmental habits quickly, before we destroy the planet.
- Economic and security crises are caused by reliance on oil and fighting over areas where there are fossil fuels, e.g., war in Iraq.
- Future generations will suffer if we use up all the world's resources.
- We should be putting more money and time into researching and developing renewable energy sources. We will only do this if we phase out the use of fossil fuels.

Possible arguments against:
- Climate change occurs whether or not we use fossil fuels.
- There are insufficient reliable alternative fuel sources to fossil fuels. We rely on fossil fuels for our standard of living in the modern world.

e)   Additional points that could be added to the debate include: the cost of doing nothing outweighs the cost of banning fossil fuels (for); opponents believe human activity has a miniscule effect on climate change (against).

Web resources

BBC Learning English: Talk about English: Insight plus
This site is aimed at English learners in an academic context and contains short talks on important issues such as globalization, global warming, etc. Each talk includes a commentary that helps you to focus on key ideas and vocabulary. Students can also download the script.
http://www.bbc.co.uk/worldservice/learningenglish/webcast/tae_insight_archive.shtml

University of Leeds: Guide to the design of questionnaires
This site gives detailed advice for each stage of designing and carrying out a survey.
http://iss.leeds.ac.uk/info/312/surveys/217/guide_to_the_design_of_questionnaires

TNJN students debate banning fossil fuels
Students can read and listen to students debating whether to ban fossil fuels.
http://tnjn.com/2008/nov/16/students-debate-banning-of-fos/

9 Thinking rationally
Science and the paranormal

In this unit students will:
- practise language for expressing differing degrees of belief;
- practise presenting a research proposal to a group of colleagues;
- consider the criteria for a good research proposal.

This unit further develops the idea of a research project as well as encouraging students to look at the assumptions behind strongly held beliefs, which in many cases reflect the underlying personal values behind attitudes.

In an academic setting it is common for postgraduate students on either Master's or PhD courses to present a proposal of their ideas for research or writing a paper.

This unit encourages students to think about a piece of research (an experiment), formulate a hypothesis and then present their idea to a group to have it evaluated.

It invites students to:
- find their own resources;
- think through the steps involved in conducting research in a methodical way;
- think critically, both as the presenters and the peer audience.

Task 1: The view of scientists

1.1 This is a series of quotations about science, made by a range of people who work in different scientific fields. Encourage students to decide their own alignment before engaging in discussion. You could ask them what aspects of science they think are the most important to teach. Some of the quotations are deliberately contrary to each other in order to provoke discussion.

Statements 1, 2 and 4 appear to support each other (uncertainty, possibility of error, humility) and contradict 2 (certainty).

1.2 You could lead into this quotation by asking students: *How do we know if something is true or false? How do we know if something exists or not?*

1.3 As an alternative to pairwork, these discussions could be set up as small-group activities. The previous discussion should have provided students with plenty to talk about.

Task 2: Beliefs that are contrary to scientific theory

2.1 Students should be able to come up with a number of ideas here. You should emphasize in this unit that the beliefs being discussed here are not religious beliefs. Do not dwell too long on this discussion, as it is a lead-in to the next discussion. However, if there is a lot of interest in it, it could be used as the basis of a presentation for some students.

2.2 Check that students understand the meaning of all these phenomena.

Definitions:

telepathy:	*Direct communication of thoughts or feelings from one person to another, using the mind, without words.*
ghosts/haunted houses:	*Spirit of a dead person wanders round; can be 'good' or 'bad'.*
mind control:	*One person being able to control the mind of another and get them to do what they want.*
hypnosis:	*An unconscious state where a person can still see and hear what is around and be influenced to follow commands.*
astrology:	*The study of the movement of the stars in order to see how this influences human events.*
fortune-telling:	*Prediction of the future of an individual through interpreting – their palm, tea-leaves, cards, etc.*
UFOs:	*Unidentified flying objects, often thought to be extraterrestrial.*
alien abductions:	*Kidnapping of humans by extraterrestrial beings.*
reincarnation:	*Return to life after death in another form, e.g., as an animal.*

You may wish to go through the *useful language* expressions before students discuss these issues. You could set it up as a group discussion of four or five students and get each group to report back briefly after the discussion. Alternatively, you could ask each group to choose five of the topics to discuss briefly.

2.3 Encourage students to come up with a range of possible explanations.

2.4/2.5 You may choose to omit these activities – or it may be that you feel these will work well with your group.

2.6 Encourage students to share ideas and give feedback to each other. Ask them to decide which is the most interesting experiment.

Task 3: Designing and presenting a research project

3.1 This activity will depend on the kind of group you have – if they are from different subject areas, emphasize that any research proposal they come up with needs to be accessible to the non-expert in the field, i.e., other students and the teacher.

Go through the following vocabulary, some of which will be familiar.

Definitions:

experimental groups:	*The experimental group receives the experimental treatment.*
control groups:	*The control group's selection and experiences are the same as the experimental group except that they do not receive the experimental treatment.*
number of subjects:	*The people who participate in the research.*
statistical significance:	*The likelihood that a result derived from a sample could have been found by chance. The more significant a result, the more likely that it represents something genuine.*
variables:	*An attribute of a person or an object which 'varies' from person to person or from object to object or from time to time.*

It is important to emphasize that students need to find out from their own departments the specific conventions for a research proposal.

If you feel it is appropriate, you can refer students to the example of a research proposal in Course Book Appendix 7, related to a Master's course in Teaching English as a Foreign Language.

3.2 Set up these presentations in a fairly formal way; the role of the audience is important here, so that they try and engage and think critically about the topic. Although the presentations will be subject-specific, clarify that they should be comprehensible to an educated audience, rather than a specialist one.

3.3 Ensure students give the presentations from notes rather than from a script.

3.4 Make copies of the feedback form at the end of this unit (Handout 4, Course Book Appendix 9g). Encourage students to give feedback using the form, paying particular attention to the first question, *How clearly did the speakers present their ideas?*

Unit summary

1 When the students have answered these questions, you might wish them to discuss their answers to give further practice in the language of expressing doubts and beliefs.

2/3 These two activities provide further practice in writing a research proposal and giving a presentation. Encourage the students to set up the presentation in their own time.

Web resources

BBC Learning English: Science vocabulary
A BBC website that explains and discusses scientific words and expressions.
http://www.bbc.co.uk/worldservice/learningenglish/grammar/vocabulary/

Audience feedback sheet (Course Book Appendix 9g)

How clearly did the speakers present their ideas?
Does it seem like a worthwhile proposal or experiment?
Can you see any problems in the experiment/proposal?
Overall comment

Photocopiable

The importance of reflection
Studying in a new environment

In this unit students will:
● practise exchanging information;
● reflect on what they have gained from their time on this course;
● reflect on the skills they have developed on the course and how they can continue to develop them.

The purpose of this unit is to get students to reflect on the course overall, and how it fits into their current scenario, thinking also about their future course of study and in particular how they will survive the next stage (most students will be in an English-speaking environment for about a year).

Task 1: Looking back

1.1/1.2 This is probably best done in three stages. For example:

1   Two minutes for students individually to note down their own ideas.
2   Three minutes for students in groups of three or four to share their ideas.
3   Three minutes for a whole-class round-up of the most interesting points.

Task 2: Stages in culture shock

2.1 This should be a useful discussion point. One way of leading into this task is to ask the class whether any of them has ever experienced 'culture shock'. If they are uncertain of the meaning of this expression, you can ask them to guess it from the constituent words.

Allow time for students in pairs or groups to discuss various possible sequences, before you tell them what in fact the original sequence was.

Answers:

Stage no.	Description of stage
4	You thought you had got used to it, but one or two minor things go wrong and it feels as if the whole world is against you. Some people give up at this stage, or become aggressive or withdrawn.
1	Excitement.
5	Adjustment to the new environment takes place. You either integrate into the new culture, or decide that you don't like it but have to tolerate it temporarily.
3	You begin to get used to it.
2	Culture shock. A few things start to go wrong. Differences between your own culture and the new culture start to cause problems. What was once new and exciting now seems unfamiliar and frustrating.

Source: Woolfenden, J. (1990). *How to study and live in Britain*. Plymouth: Northcote House.

2.2 Monitor the discussion. If group members do not feel (in their discussion of questions a and b) that Woolfenden's five stages correspond to their own experience at all, ask them to try to outline an alternative series of stages that do reflect their own experience.

2.3 The 'difficult stages' are presumably Stage 2 and Stage 4. This question anticipates the content of Task 3, where students listen to advice from people who have just completed their courses.

Task 3: Listening to cultural advice

This is a jigsaw listening task.

The texts are adapted from interviews with an MA student of Applied Linguistics and a native-English MSc student of Agricultural Extension and Rural Development. If you have anyone in your class who is particularly interested in either of these fields, you can steer her/him towards the appropriate listening text.

3.1 🎧 **17/18** Prepare students for the listening task by directing them to the rubric in the Course Book and eliciting some possible examples of 'the challenges that face international students'. If the opportunity arises here, pre-teach language items that you think might otherwise present problems for your students in the listening texts.

3.2 You could pair weaker students with stronger students to ensure each individual has the key points noted down.

3.3 Monitor students' notes and discussions during the exchange of information, to ensure that they are on the right lines.

3.4 Get students to present their ranking briefly.

Task 4: Advice for international students

4.1 Students could work in groups of four. Encourage them to think about how they felt when they first arrived, and what they found most useful in helping them to settle in – what kind of information was it useful to have?

4.2 You may want to set this for homework, depending on the facilities available to you in class.

4.3 You can let the students decide on the representative for the group.

4.4 Model advice sheets can be found in Appendix 2I.

Task 5: Assessing your progress

Encourage students to look back through the course materials to remind themselves of the areas covered during the course. They should look at any feedback sheets they have received during the course from peers or teachers.

Get students to re-read their learner diary entries and encourage them to reflect on their progress throughout.

Get students to focus on the areas they have made progress in, emphasizing the positive aspects of their learning.

Task 6: Ideas for future study

Encourage students to be practical and concrete about how they can continue to develop their spoken English.

Web resources

BBC Learning English: Talk about English: Who on earth are we?
This is a collection of 12 programmes for English learners that look at and explain the theory behind cultural differences. The programmes look at areas such as culture shock, cultural misunderstandings and the differences between individualist and collectivist cultures.
http://www.bbc.co.uk/worldservice/learningenglish/webcast/tae_whoonearth_archive.shtml

Unit 1: Communicating in academic situations

Track 1 (1:31)
Ex 2.3

Listen to another group of students reporting back on their discussion of the points in Ex 2.1. Which statements do they refer to?

1

Student A: Our group thought the most controversial point was the first one – wanting to speak English with a native-speaker accent.

2

Student B: Point 'd', concerning the importance of grammar and pronunciation, provoked the most discussion in our group. Some people felt that grammar was more important than pronunciation, but others disagreed strongly.

3

Student A: Point 'f' was the most controversial point of discussion in our group; people were very divided over the issue of working in groups affecting their grammatical accuracy.

4

Student B: There was some disagreement about point 'g', the point about speaking English for social reasons, but most of the group agreed that international students will need to communicate socially.

Track 2 (1:57)
Ex 3.2

Listen to two students discussing these statements. Does the second speaker agree, disagree or partly agree with each statement?

a)

Speaker A: If you want to succeed at university, you really need to manage your time well.

Speaker B: Absolutely. I totally agree, because otherwise you will fall behind.

b)

Speaker A: It's important to do a lot of reading around before you choose a focus for your essays.

Speaker B: Yes, that's true, but you need to limit the amount you read.

c)

Speaker A: The best time to revise for exams is just before the exam, when the pressure is on.

Speaker B: I'm not sure I agree with you there. Many people can't think clearly under pressure.

d)

Speaker A: The same study skills are necessary on both undergraduate and postgraduate courses.

Speaker B: I agree up to a point, but postgraduates probably need more developed research skills.

e)

Speaker A: If you've completed an academic course in one country, you should be able to cope with a course in another country.

Speaker B: Not necessarily. There are different academic cultures in different countries. You may have to learn a new approach to studying.

f)

Speaker A: People have different learning styles. It helps you learn more quickly if you're aware of how you learn best.

Speaker B: That's a very good point. It can really help you to study more efficiently if you understand your own strengths and weaknesses.

Track 3 (4:58)
Ex 4.1

Listen and number the points below according to the order in which the students discuss them.

Sarah: Hi Majid, how are you doing?

Majid: Yes, I am fine, and you Sarah?

Sarah: I'm fine, I haven't seen you in ages. How is your course going now?

Majid: It's just so much, to be honest. So much.

Sarah: Are you really busy?

Majid: Yes, really, really busy.

Sarah: I'm in my final year now and I have an awful lot of work on. I do History and it is so much reading.

Majid: Yes, it's the same, you know. I am doing Applied Linguistics and it is just beyond my head. It's so much reading.

Sarah: How do you cope with all the reading?

Majid: I try just to prioritize my reading lists. This is what I do. I read on a daily basis – I am not sure – as a native speaker maybe that is not your technique, is it?

Sarah: Well, being a native-speaking student, I try to leave my reading to the last minute. But how do you pick out the relevant bits in your reading list? As a History student I get a list as long as my arm of different books to read by different people, and sometimes you don't know what's important. How do you do that?

Majid: I try just to focus on my lecture and after the lecture I ask my tutor which book would be very easy to read and give me a very good introduction about the topic. Otherwise I would just end up wasting my time searching for books that are relevant.

Sarah: Same here. I always try to speak to my tutor or my lecturer and ask them what is the best title to read. And also, because I do a subject where I have to write a lot of essays and a lot of analytical writing, I also try to ask them about who is on which side of the debate and who would give the best answer to a question.

Majid: Yes, that is a very good idea. Do you mean that you try to ask your tutor about which book or what kind of writer each writer is, I mean try to understand the argument first?

Sarah: My course is an awful lot about different theories and different approaches to events that happened in the past and so it is very important when I look at my reading list to be able to see who said what about an event. So that helps a lot. But still it takes an awful lot of time.

Majid: Yes, and how do you manage your time?

Sarah: How do you, first?

Majid: I have to be honest because the reading is very difficult. I try to finish an article very quickly and follow the techniques that we learnt in the pre-sessional course, for example like skimming and scanning, and read the abstract first, things like this. And that is just to help me to cope with the time.

Sarah: I wish that they had taught us all these little handy hints and tips. As a native-speaking student they just expect you to know what to do.

Majid: Hmm!

Sarah: And, with, you know, trying to manage your time as well as all this reading, you've got all these essays and presentations to do throughout the term and sometimes you feel that you have got so much going on, there's an awful lot of stress. How do you manage stress?

Majid: It's very difficult this, a killer to be honest, and sometimes I just leave it and just have a chat with a friend or just relax sometimes, you know?

Sarah: With the university course, generally they are not very consistent. Some weeks you may have presentations and essays to do and some weeks you may have only a bit of reading. I find it helps to manage your time by, say, doing something before you have to do it, doing reading before you have to do it and also essays as well. Do you find that doing an essay early helps?

Majid: Yes, that's what I do. I start very early. I do a kind of a plan before I start my essay and then I send it to my tutor and I ask him if it's a good plan or not and can I start writing in that topic if the plan is okay. And they usually give you very good feedback, and after the feedback I start reading and writing and try to finish very early. And when you finish your essays, how do you edit them well, what kinds of things do you do to them?

Sarah: When I write an essay, I try to write it in parts, but I don't know if this is a very good technique, it is just what I've done for many years. Once I have finished an essay, I read it and then I get someone else to read it, to make sure it makes sense and that it is not just made-up stuff in my head that doesn't make any sense at all. It is very important to have someone else read your work before you hand it in. Because especially in extended writing, where it is your thoughts going down on paper, it is very important that it makes sense.

Majid: Do you choose the topic that you are going to write about?

Sarah: Yes, it is very important when you choose any course that you are interested and want to do it. It must be even more important as a non-native speaker to be interested in what you are doing, so that you have the drive to keep going and persevere when things are hard.

Track 4 (1:20)

Ex 6.1

Now listen to a student presenting his top five study tips. Are any of the points the same as yours?

Student: There are five main points which we consider important for successful study.

Our first point is you need to be well-organized. Without this, you will not be able to manage all the work you are given.

Next, we have put the importance of working with classmates. Students often need to cooperate with each other in seminars and planning presentations.

Moving onto our third point, keep good notes. There is so much information to deal with from both lectures and reading that you need to take notes effectively and reread these.

Fourthly, we think that good IT skills are now an essential part of university study. Students often need to use the Internet for research purposes, so they need to know how to search for useful information.

And finally, our last point is the importance of motivation – you really need to want to learn about your subject. If not, you will find it hard to study if you are just not interested in it.

Unit 2: Seminars and discussions

Track 5 (1:28)

Ex 2.3

Now listen to a student comparing different perspectives on the statement in Ex 2.1. What does the speaker say about the views of those involved?

Student: From a teacher's perspective, he or she would probably be concerned about the effect of the child's behaviour on other children – how it might negatively affect their progress and learning – so would probably want the child excluded from school.

From the point of view of the parents, they would say it was the teacher's and school's responsibility to deal with the child's behaviour problems and that excluding the child was an easy way out for the school. They would say that the child should remain and the school should work out a solution.

If I were the headteacher of the child's school, I'd probably feel that the reputation of the school might be damaged by excluding the child. It might give the school a bad name as people might think it was a problem school. As a headteacher, I'd want the child to remain at the school, despite the problems.

The child psychologist would argue that we need to understand and deal with the cause of the child's bad behaviour, and that excluding the child would not do that. In fact, it might damage the child more.

Track 6 (0:48)

Ex 4.1

Listen to a student summarizing a group discussion of the statement from Ex 2.1 relating to the exclusion of disruptive children. Did the group agree or disagree with the statement?

Student: This is a difficult question, but we finally all agreed that such a child should be excluded from school, as this would be in the best interests of most people concerned. It's true that this action might cause some damage to the child's long-term ability to socialize effectively with other children, so we also agreed that this action should only be taken if there is no other solution, I mean, if all else fails.

Track 7 (1:30)
Ex 4.4

Listen to a student using some of the phrases.

Student: After much consideration, we decided that corporal punishment is not really necessary to maintain discipline in schools.

All things considered, we felt that children should not leave school until they are 18.

On balance, we felt that parents should not be allowed to educate their children at home.

We couldn't reach agreement on this issue. Some of us felt that corporal punishment is necessary, whilst others disagreed strongly.

We recognized that there are some disadvantages for the child, such as pressure and stress, but we still felt exams at a young age are a good idea.

We're fully aware that lack of discipline in schools is a major problem. However, we still felt that corporal punishment is not the answer.

One has to acknowledge that some parents could educate their children very well. We still felt, however, that only parents with teaching qualifications should be allowed to do this by law.

So, although we agreed with the statement, we stressed that children of 15 should receive careful advice on which subjects to choose.

Unit 3: Examining underlying assumptions

Track 8 (3:15)
Ex 3.3

Listen to a student presenting key points from the same article.

Student: As the title suggests, this article deals with an apparent change in the role men would like to play in family life. First of all, it provides some statistics to support this claim, then looks at two issues related to it: the decline in the social stigma attached to being a stay-at-home dad and the question of the resources needed to support men who choose this new role.

So, the article reports that increasing numbers of men would prefer to stop working or work less in order to look after their children and home. It refers to statistics from the government, which show that 200,000 men now stay at home full-time to look after their children.

The article also gives statistics from a magazine survey of 2,000 couples. As you can see, only one-third of those asked, 34 per cent in fact, wanted to continue working full-time after having children. The majority either wanted to return to part-time work or become full-time househusbands. This is what the men in the poll said they wanted. According to the article, however, what stops them from actually giving up work and staying at home is, not surprisingly, money or worries about money.

The article then goes on to say that the social stigma attached to men stopping work to bring up a family is disappearing … social stigma – this means something people might be ashamed of doing, that society would not approve of. As I said, this is disappearing, so you now see more men coming to schools and playgroups to collect their children.

Finally, the article argues that more resources are needed to support these new full-time fathers, such as this website www.homedad.org.uk. It quotes a founder of the website as saying that most current resources for parents are aimed at mothers. So, the article reports on some interesting changes in social attitudes to work and fatherhood. However, it doesn't mention the effect of socioeconomic background on men's decisions or wishes regarding work and parenthood. I mean, the men who are choosing or wanting to give up work to become househusbands, are these men from high, middle or lower income groups? We don't know this from the text, but this could be significant data.

Track 9 (1:47)
Ex 3.5

Listen to the three extracts and underline where the speaker slows down and stresses particular words or phrases.

Extract 1

Student: The article also gives statistics from a magazine survey of 2,000 couples. As you can see, only one-third of those asked, 34 per cent in fact, wanted to continue working full-time after having children. The majority either wanted to return to part-time work or become full-time househusbands.

Extract 2

Student: The article then goes on to say that the social stigma attached to men stopping work to bring up a family is disappearing … social stigma – this means something people might be ashamed of doing, that society would not approve of. As I said, this is disappearing, so you now see more men coming to schools and playgroups to collect their children.

Extract 3

Student: So, the article reports on some interesting changes in social attitudes to work and fatherhood. However, it doesn't mention the effect of socioeconomic background on men's decisions or wishes regarding work and parenthood. I mean, the men who are choosing or wanting to give up work to become househusbands, are these men from high, middle or lower income groups?

Track 10 (1:14)
Ex 5.4

Listen to some students exchanging opinions on different topics. Tick the expressions you hear.

1

Student A:	It seems to me that women are being forced to have careers when they really want to stay at home.
Student B:	I take your point, but don't you think that's making an assumption that all women want to have children?

2

Student A:	In my view, women are biologically designed to bring up children, and men to be the breadwinners.
Student B:	Well, I think that is a rather old-fashioned idea.

3

Student A:	Just because it's traditional or normal for women to stay at home, doesn't necessarily mean it's natural.
Student B:	I understand what you're saying, but you have to consider this question from the perspective of different cultures.

4

Student A:	Women are built differently, and are not suitable for certain jobs, such as engineering and construction.
Student B:	Well, I'm not sure if that's quite true – you need to consider the reality, that in fact a number of women are employed in the construction industry.

Unit 4: Reading into speaking

Track 11 (1:50)
Ex 4.2

Listen to some of these expressions in context. Tick the ones which you hear.

1

Student A:	It's not really up to the government to do something about smoking, is it? Why do we always expect the government to deal with these sorts of issues, rather than making smokers themselves face up to the problem?
Student B:	So what you're saying is that there is no point in the government trying to tackle the problem of smoking until individuals take responsibility for their own health …

2

Student A:	I don't see why this subject gets so much attention. People have always had to work hard and I'm sure it will continue like that. If you're organized, it shouldn't be a problem.
Student B:	So in your view, dealing with stress is not a major issue; people just need to manage their time properly …

3

Student A:	So as far as I'm concerned, it needs to be approached from the perspective of having a healthy and happy lifestyle … do you understand what I mean?
Student B:	Yes, absolutely.

4

Student A: The fast food industry is only concerned with making a profit. It will mislead the public about what's in the junk food they sell. It can't be left to police itself.

Student B: I'm not sure I understand what you mean.

Student A: What I'm saying is that the fast food industry is not concerned about people's health. They just want to make money, so they won't tell the truth about what they put in hamburgers, for example. The government needs to pass laws controlling what can be put in junk food. You can't just leave it to the fast food industry to decide.

Unit 5: The use of data

Track 12 (1:07)
Ex 3.2

Listen to the description of the data shown and answer the following questions.

Speaker: This graph shows monthly visits to the cinema by age groups between 1984 and 2003.

As you can see, young people aged between 15 and 24 are the most likely age group to go to the cinema. Fifty-four per cent of this age group attended the cinema once a month or more in Great Britain in 2003. In 2003, 39 per cent of children aged seven to 14 went to the cinema once a month or more, as can be seen from this line here. The percentage for both these age groups has risen noticeably since 1984.

From this data, it is clear that going to the cinema is still a popular form of entertainment, despite the arrival of videos, DVDs and computer games.

Track 13 (7:49)
Ex 4.1

You are going to hear a journalist talking about the BBC.

Interviewer: So Paul, can you tell us a little bit about how the BBC got started initially?

BBC employee: The BBC was set up in 1922. Um, its first director general was a 33-year-old Scottish engineer called John Reith, who was invited to become the first director and his vision, it is important to know this guy's name, John Reith, his vision was very important for the establishing of the BBC. His vision of what it should be was very, very influential. Um, basically he had a phrase which he used which was to inform, educate and entertain. And these were the three pillars of what he thought the BBC should do.

Interviewer: Mmm.

BBC employee: Inform, educate and entertain, in that order. It is interesting that educate comes before entertain.

Interviewer: Indeed, yes.

BBC employee: Yes, in his vision of it, and this kind of motto is still used in the BBC today, inform, educate and entertain, and it can still be seen in something that is called the Reith Lectures that happen every year. Radio lectures on an important scientific or cultural issue of the day which are dedicated to Lord Reith, the first director general.

Interviewer: And was it accepted from very early on that the BBC would be an independent organization editorially?

BBC employee: Yes, um, that is very interesting, um, John Reith's vision was that the BBC should be financially independent and editorially independent. Financially, well he had seen the commercial radio being set up in the USA and commercial radio was basically paid for by the advertising. So the advertisers had a lot of power and he had seen other European broadcasters being set up, who were controlled by the government, and so there was a lot of political influence over them. And he wanted something that would be completely separate from both of them, and that was his vision.

He was tested very early on, actually, in 1926, only four years after the BBC was set up there was the General Strike. This took place during the Great Depression of the 20s and everybody was on strike. Newspapers weren't being printed, people couldn't get information and the Home Secretary at the time, Mr Winston Churchill, tried to use the BBC to broadcast government propaganda. But John Reith was very, very strict about this, absolutely refused to broadcast what he saw as government propaganda and tried to broadcast independently what the BBC thought was actually happening, and I guess this was the beginning of the BBC's reputation for total independence in its news reporting.

Interviewer: Yes, I mean one of the most admirable qualities of the BBC has been its ability to maintain its independence and, um, I am wondering if this has been challenged in various, if it is still being challenged over this.

BBC employee: The BBC's political independence has been challenged constantly over its history, really. Especially in the last twenty years, it has been attacked by both right-wing and left-wing political parties. In the 1980s, Margaret Thatcher and the Conservative Party used to call it the Bolshevik Broadcasting Company. Bolshevik as in the Russian Revolution, they claimed it was very biased and very left-wing. And in 2003, the left-wing party, the Labour Party, had a very serious falling out with the BBC over the Iraq war. What became known as the Kelly Affair. Basically the BBC claimed in a radio programme that the government had deliberately exaggerated the threat from Saddam Hussein's Iraq in order to persuade the public to go to war with Iraq. The government denied that they had been misleading the public. They were very angry about the BBC's report and the scientist at the centre of this big argument, who had actually given the information to the BBC, unfortunately committed suicide, and there was a great big argument, big public investigation about this, and in the end the judge who was leading the investigation, decided for the government and against the BBC, and the BBC had to apologize and the leader, actually the director general at the time actually, resigned, although a lot of the general public didn't agree with this ruling.

Interviewer: Absolutely, yes.

BBC employee: It was a very serious setback for the BBC.

Interviewer: Yes, and it was very evident in the march to London when one million people took to the streets to demonstrate against the government.

BBC employee: Certainly, yeah, and that had to be reported just by the BBC just as much as the propaganda for going to war with Iraq was reported, and they both had to be reported in a balanced way.

Interviewer: Yes, so in many ways the BBC has been a very controversial organization throughout the ages since it started.

BBC employee: It certainly has.

Interviewer: I am wondering how it manages to finance itself throughout all of this.

BBC employee: Well, the BBC has a special, I think unique, form of financing at the moment, where it gets money from people, from everybody who has a TV. If you have a TV in your house you must pay a licence for it every year, and that includes students. That might be some of your students might need to get one. The licences are £139.50, I think, and …

Interviewer: Quite a substantial amount!

BBC Employee: Quite a substantial amount, which you have to pay every year and this money is used for making radio and TV programmes. The BBC has other ways of making money and it sells its programmes abroad to other channels, it makes books which tie in with its programmes and it has various merchandising branches, but it doesn't carry advertising. The only advertising you will see on the BBC is for other BBC programmes.

Interviewer: Yes, yes. And it is one of the reasons why people opt to watch BBC rather than other channels.

BBC employee: Some people find it very refreshing not to have to have advertisements every 15 minutes.

Interviewer: Yes, especially in the middle of films.

And the BBC still does continue to play a very important role in people's lives. Very often at lunchtime, breaktime, you will hear people talking about a programme that they had seen on television.

BBC employee: Yes, the BBC plays an integral part in British life. People have grown up with it for generations. There are soap operas on BBC radio which are 50 years old. It is the oldest soap opera in the world. It is the nation's favourite information source. Most people still get their information from the BBC. The BBC is still the most trusted organization in the country.

Interviewer: So why do you think the BBC still plays such an important role in British life? I mean, very often at lunchtime, the topic of conversation would be a programme that people have watched the night before.

BBC employee: Absolutely, I think the BBC still plays an integral part in British life. People have grown up with it for generations. It is like a trusted friend. It is still where people get most of their information from. Certainly, the BBC is more trusted than any politician and people are very protective of it. They don't like to see the BBC being attacked by politicians. I also think people are very proud of the BBC. They see broadcasting as something that we still do well in this country. The BBC itself still claims that it is the second most recognized brand name in the world, after Coca-Cola.

Interviewer: *[laughs]* And it certainly offers us a lot more than Coca-Cola does! Thank you very much, Paul.

BBC employee: Thank you.

Interviewer: Very informative.

Track 14 (2:53)
Ex 5.3

Listen to three students discussing freedom of speech and answer the following questions.

Student A: I don't think you can really put any limits on freedom of speech. It should be an absolute principle in a mature democracy, don't you think?

Student B: When you say 'an absolute principle', do you mean that anyone can say or broadcast or print anything they want to about anyone else on any subject?

Student A: Yes, I think so. Obviously, you expect that people will use that right responsibly and not use it in a way that will lead to violence or worse.

Student C: Yes, I think I agree. I mean, once you start putting limits on freedom of speech, then it's a dangerous road to go down. As you said, it's a fundamental part of a democratic society. If those in authority start restricting that right, if those in power have the right to decide what can or can't be said, then I think it's a dangerous sort of power to have. You made an interesting point about using the right to freedom of speech in a responsible way. That's what I think a mature democracy should be based on – people have the right to free speech, but are responsible enough not to abuse it, not to exercise it in a negative way.

Student B: Yes, but following on from that point, that's where I have a problem with the idea of an absolute right to freedom of speech, particularly regarding what you both say about responsibility and mature democracies. The reality is people can't be trusted to use that right in a responsible way. Why should people have the right to make racist comments or things which might cause violence against others or whatever? Can I also pick up on your point about not allowing those in power to limit freedom of speech? I mean, I would have thought that in a mature democracy, yes, those in power must listen to the majority, but they also need to protect minorities, and that means limiting the rights of people to say things in public which might put those minority groups in danger.

Student A: OK, those are fair arguments, but you make the point that a society needs to protect minority groups, but if the government can limit freedom of speech, they might start silencing minority groups and that's not protecting them. There might be less tolerance of different, non-majority views and opinions.

Student C: Exactly.

Student B: I know, it's not an easy question, but I still think that a society in which anyone can say anything may in fact lead to a less tolerant society than one where there are some limits on what you can say. As I said before, people might use free speech to take away the freedom of other people to feel safe in a society.

Student C: I think we'll have to agree to disagree on this issue.

Unit 7: Supporting your point of view

Track 15 (6:54)
Ex 4.4

Listen to the interview.

Interviewer: Good morning, Sonia. You've done some research into the role of women in the construction industry specifically. Can I start, however, by asking you about the participation of women in the labour market more generally? What are the reasons why more women are participating in the labour market?

Sonia Gurjao: The main reasons for women's increased participation in the labour market would be the deskilling of historically male jobs. Secondly, demographics have changed. We have an increased life expectancy and women today tend to have fewer children than they did in the past. We also have a restructuring of psychological expectations, such as women's own expectations of themselves and what they want to do in life and today, in today's day and age, it's become an economic necessity to have two incomes in a family to be able to support a family and to be able to accommodate the general running of the house.

Interviewer: Is that because of the cost of living?

Sonia Gurjao: Yes, that is because of the increased cost of living today. And another reason is women are more highly educated today than they have ever been in the past. And all these factors contribute towards their increased participation in the labour market.

Interviewer: Now, moving on to the construction industry itself. Is the construction industry a common career choice for women?

Sonia Gurjao: No, actually, the construction industry is not an obvious career choice for women. In fact, lots of women are not informed about the construction industry as a career of choice. This starts right from schools, where they aren't informed of construction, science, engineering and technology subjects as a choice that they could do or pursue as their career choices. And one of the reasons is the construction industry also has a bad image, that is one related to hard work, and working in extreme conditions. It's known as the dirty industry and it's not attractive to women as such.

Interviewer: As I understand it, from your research, the construction industry does need more women though to join it? Why is that?

Sonia Gurjao: The construction industry plays a critical role in Britain's prosperity and it employs over two million people, and in the past it had a steady choice of entrants into the industry, probably because of the way people chose their careers and people pursued vocational training, but with the change in the education system and people pursuing higher education, the traditional source of labour doesn't tend to go into vocational training and so we now see a skills shortage in the construction industry. And with 50 per cent of the labour participation being women, today for the construction industry, including women within construction becomes a very important aspect.

Interviewer: Has the construction industry itself made any attempts to try to recruit women into the industry?

Sonia Gurjao: The construction industry has not actively gone into recruiting women, but as they've seen, and as the government's seen that there's going to be a problem with recruiting your traditional force of labour, they've started looking into recruiting women as a solution to the labour problems and also making the construction industry more inclusive and looking for talent from the other 50 per cent of the labour workforce. So, what they've done is they've gone to schools and they have projects where they encourage young girls to do, like they have little training sessions and they have workshops where they actively participate and build things to encourage them or to show them what working in the construction industry might be like.

Interviewer: So, they've gone to the schools …

Sonia Gurjao: They've started from school levels and then they have, even for young people, they've started for career advisors, they've started training career advisors into encouraging or to stop stereotyping career choices for young people.

Interviewer: And that's to try and encourage young girls …

Sonia Gurjao: Not just young girls, but to also encourage boys as well into construction. Because it's not only girls who lack interest in the construction industry, it is also the lack of men in the construction industry.

Interviewer: I understand that the industry has a problem with keeping women who join the construction industry. Why is that and is there a solution to this problem?

Sonia Gurjao: I think that's a recent realization from the part of the industry. They have a long-working-hour culture because of the kind of projects there are, because they tend to be projects that need to be deadlines, because of the cost involved in the projects as well. So, ultimately what happens is when you have women who are 50 per cent of the workforce, but then out of these 50 per cent of the workforce, around 44 per cent of women actually only work part-time and the industry doesn't have part-time working, so that makes it difficult for women to be present in the industry, to be working. So that's where the industry has started realizing that if we have to recruit women we have to make an attempt to be flexible, as in other industries like telecommunications and banking, which have of course benefited from making their jobs flexible.

Interviewer: Could you just summarize what you see to be the main barriers which women face today in joining or staying in the construction industry?

Sonia Gurjao: What we repeatedly hear in the past is that the construction industry is dirty, dangerous and not suitable for women. But in today's day and age, where technology has taken over and we have more managing of projects and we have consultancy, so in today's construction industry, the main barriers would actually be flexible working in terms of 44 per cent of women actually working part-time in the labour force participation. If we need to target that, we need to make the industry more flexible and it needs to see that people need to have a better work/life balance and organizations need to change to accommodate this.

Unit 8: Collecting and presenting data

Track 16 (0:50)
Ex 4.2

Listen to a student using *useful language* expressions from Ex 1.5. Underline the words or phrases in the box which the speaker uses.

1   Most of the respondents claimed that they take recycling seriously and recycled glass, plastic and paper products.

2   Approximately a third of those interviewed were prepared to be part of a car-sharing scheme.

3   Just over 50 per cent of the subjects said that they would buy environmentally-friendly products even if those products were more expensive.

Track 17 (7:57)

Ex 3.1

Listen to a speaker who recently completed a postgraduate degree at a British university.

Text 1

EAP tutor: Hello, Gulin. Thanks for agreeing to come and talk about the experience of studying here as an international student. You're just finishing a one-year Masters course, aren't you?

Gulin: Yes, that's right.

EAP tutor: What has it been like for you, working with British and other international students together?

Gulin: Well, it has been a new kind of experience for me. Everything was new to me at the beginning. But as in any new situation, I gradually learnt to adapt. I think that, if you're studying at a university with people from all over the world, then you need to accept that there will be cultural differences between people and you need to be tolerant of them so that you can get along with people well enough to work with them. Oh, and of course, it's right to expect other people to show a similar acceptance and tolerance towards you.

EAP tutor: Yes, I know that students are sometimes advised to form study groups with others on the course. Did you do that, and, if so, was it helpful?

Gulin: Yes, I agree that it's a good idea. But of course it doesn't work with just anybody. I think it's worth looking for people who have similar study habits to your own, and if possible people who don't live too far away from you. And, again, you have to be prepared to be flexible; to adjust your own approach a little sometimes, so that it's easier for other people to work with you.

EAP tutor: Now, what about the tutor? When you started your course, was it clear to you how to approach the tutor and what for?

Gulin: I think the responsibilities of the tutor are written in the department's handbook.

EAP tutor: That's good.

Gulin: So the student should read that to get a basic idea of the support she is entitled to expect from her tutor. But you need to play it by ear a little at first, because obviously tutors are human and so they're different. You have to approach different tutors in different ways. One point I would make about meetings with your tutor is: it is worth preparing a little bit before the meeting – working out the questions you want to ask and the kind of answers you expect or need, so that you make the best possible use of the time during the meeting. Personally, I take in a list of points in order of priority: like 1, 2, 3, 4, etc.

EAP tutor: Apart from your tutor and fellow students, what other resources have you made use of during your period of study?

Gulin:	Well, I would advise any new student to explore the university campus thoroughly early on in her stay, if possible with some guidance from a more experienced student to get to know the facilities that are available. The first place I explored was the library – it's important to find which parts of the library are particularly relevant to your subject area, and to discover whether there are other, specialist libraries or collections in some departments. For example, in my case, there were books on linguistics in one part of the main library, periodicals in the other part, and then there was the departmental library and also a useful library in a neighbouring college. It took a while to discover where everything was.
	But the library is not the only facility which is open to all students from all departments: some departments or units run an advisory service. This means that at certain times of the day students from any department can go along and ask for help with their project. It's well worthwhile asking about these advisory services early on in your course, and don't be afraid to make use of them – they are there to help students, that's their function.
EAP tutor:	Did you use these advisory services yourself?
Gulin:	Oh, yes, two of them. The advisory service in the Computer Centre has helped me several times: once when my disk was stuck, and another time when I thought I'd lost a lot of data … And the Applied Statistics Department also runs an advisory service, which I'd recommend to anyone who's going to do experimental research. The staff there will discuss the design of your experiment with you – of course, you should do this early on in your project at the planning stage, so that it's not too late to make any changes that they suggest. They will also help you to analyze the data later on.
EAP tutor:	Right. The facilities you've mentioned so far have been broadly academic. What other kinds would you advise new students to make use of?
Gulin:	They should make use of the Students' Union, of course; after all, it is supposed to be run by the students for the students. It has an Overseas Students Committee, which is made up of people who have already been in the UK for a year or two and want to use their experience to improve the services provided for overseas students. You can contact them at the Students' Union.
	Another good reason for visiting the Union, as well as the shops, is that it's the information centre for various university clubs or groups, and for student activities in general. In one part of the building there are several big noticeboards, where groups can advertise forthcoming events and sometimes a list for people to sign up if they are interested in a particular activity. There are also boards for other kinds of notice: for example, people who want to share accommodation, or second-hand books for sale.
EAP tutor:	I imagine those groups are a good way for overseas students to meet British students, for social reasons and also perhaps to practise speaking English.
Gulin:	Yeah, I agree.
EAP tutor:	Did you do that yourself? Did you join one of these clubs?
Gulin:	Oh yeah, I joined the Chess Club. That was a good move, because sometimes you need a place where you can get right away from your academic studies for a while. Chess is always refreshing; you sit down and … I guess you use a different part of the brain. And as well as the chess itself, there is the social contact. People tend to talk a lot at our chess evenings; maybe not so much during, but before and after their games; not just about chess – all kinds of things.

EAP tutor:	And what about sports? I know there are quite a lot of sports clubs advertised on the noticeboards as well.
Gulin:	Yeah, there are various sports, and the one I'm interested in is mountaineering …
EAP tutor:	Mountaineering!
Gulin:	Yeah. It can be quite demanding, but it gives you a sense of satisfaction when you climb … the highest mountain in Wales, for example.
EAP tutor:	I'll have to take your word for that. Right, finally, is there any advice that you wish you'd had at the beginning of your course?
Gulin:	Yes, to be prepared for a style of lecture in which contributions from the audience are often invited by the lecturer. If you are not used to this style, it can at first seem off-putting, even aggressive. Try to practise contributing so that you can join in the discussion.
	Perhaps I should explain that, although contributions to the class discussion were encouraged, it was certainly not acceptable for a student to engage in private discussion with the one or two people nearest to him during a lecture. That happened a couple of times in the first week of my course, and it was an irritating distraction for the lecturer and all the other students.
	One final point: make an effort to see the course as a whole from the start. If, as in my case, the most important part of the course in terms of both assessment and learning is a dissertation project, use the early parts of the course to prepare for the dissertation. Jot down ideas about it from time to time, to help you gradually work towards it.
EAP tutor:	Right, well, thank you very much, Gulin. You've been very helpful.
Gulin:	It was a pleasure.

Track 18 (6:12)
Ex 3.1

Listen to a speaker who recently completed a postgraduate degree at a British university.

Text 2

EAP tutor:	Now, Chris, can I get this right? You've just completed an MSc course on which a large proportion of the students were international students? Is that right?
Chris:	That's it. Yes, I was in AERD – that's the Department of Agricultural Extension and Rural Development.
EAP tutor:	And how do you think the students from other countries got on on that course?
Chris:	Pretty well. I think we found as the course went on that we were all in the same boat really. For example, the majority of both home and international students were returning to full-time study after several years in work. That was an important thing to have in common.
EAP tutor:	What advice would you give students, particularly international students, based on your experience as a student here?

Chris: I think the most basic thing is to make use, full use, of your tutors and lecturers. Maybe some of the overseas students, perhaps even some of the home students, don't do that. They're a bit too shy early on of taking questions or problems to tutors or of making use of the time that tutors make available. So, the first piece of advice I'd give, I think, is to find out at the beginning of your course the times at which your tutor is going to be available for tutorial appointments, and then make full use of them.

EAP tutor: So, any problems, they should tell the tutor as soon as possible?

Chris: Yes.

EAP tutor: And, of course, if they're in a department where they don't have a personal tutor, I suppose they could go to the lecturer concerned. Moving on, what about the amount of reading that you have to do as a university student?

Chris: Yes! It looked pretty daunting at first, with those long reading lists. I think the important point here is to be selective: don't think you have to read everything that's listed – you're not expected to. Find which are the most important items on the list – ask the lecturer or tutor if necessary, and then, if your time is limited, spend it reading those books thoroughly.

EAP tutor: What about study resources on the campus – the library, for example. Any tips there?

Chris: Yes, make use of the recall system. If, when you get to the library, you find that the particular books you need have been borrowed by someone else, don't give up. Fill out a recall slip, hand it in at the information desk, and within a few days the library will contact you to tell you the book is now ready to collect. Once I discovered this system, unfortunately not until halfway through my course, I used it a lot and I found it very helpful. Of course, it means you need to plan your work properly; it's no good leaving the essential reading for an assignment until just before the deadline, and then trying to use the recall system – it's too late then.

EAP tutor: Any advice on working with other students?

Chris: When you are given an assignment, definitely talk to your fellow students about it: discuss your initial ideas about it, and then later how you're getting on with it, what you're finding difficult, etc. This will help you to think around the topic, and will also reassure you that you are not the only person feeling the strain.

And if you feel keen, you can try setting up a study group with some of the others. On our course, for example, five of us formed a study group in the second term and worked together on revising for the exams. But a study group can be helpful at any point in the course – for a particular assignment, for instance. You need to work out which of the other students on your course you find it easy to work with, maybe people who have the same approach to study as you, or simply people who live in the same hall of residence as you. I got together with four others and we decided that we could do the reading for the exams more enjoyably and more efficiently by sharing it. So we agreed which person should read which item on the list, and then we met up once or twice a week after lectures and summarized our reading for each other. And when someone wasn't clear about something, or disagreed with something, we discussed it. I learnt a lot from that. It also made me more confident about expressing my ideas, as you need to do in seminars.

EAP tutor: So, try to form a study group with other students to share the workload.

Chris: Yes.

EAP tutor:	Now, what about choosing options? That's often a very important part of a course, making selections about exactly what you will study. Any advice there?
Chris:	One point I would make is, perhaps it's obvious: choose options according to which subject interests you, not according to who the lecturer is. Don't choose an option simply because it's organized by someone who gives nice, clear lectures. There may be a greater risk of some overseas students making this mistake because they are so concerned about understanding every word of a lecture. But we all agreed, at the end of our course, that the subject, not the lecturer, should be the most important consideration when you choose options. If you choose a subject that really interests you, it is quite likely to provide you with a dissertation topic that you are really motivated to work on.
EAP tutor:	Right, well that's …
Chris:	So, go for the subject not the lecturer.
EAP tutor:	That's my next question, actually! Any advice on writing the dissertation – if you're a postgraduate – or an extended essay if you're an undergraduate?
Chris:	As soon as you have drafted a proposal, an outline of what you intend to write about, have a meeting with your tutor or supervisor to establish whether the basic idea is viable. This is important because otherwise you might spend days working on a project, only to discover at a later stage that a supervisor has some basic objection to what you're doing, and you have wasted a lot of time. So, have an early meeting to get some official feedback on your proposal.
	One other point about working on a major project, such as a dissertation: draw up a work schedule at the beginning, with reasonable deadlines by which you intend to complete each stage of the project. The project can seem like a huge mountain to climb at first, so it's good for morale if you divide it up into manageable sections: 'I'll finish reading by the end of April, I'll complete data collection by mid-May, and then I'll write the first two chapters by the end of May'; that kind of thing. Even if you don't meet all the deadlines, you will have a sense of progress.
EAP tutor:	OK, that's very helpful, Chris. Thank you very much.
Chris:	Not at all.

Appendices

Appendix 1: Useful language

The photocopiable *useful language* expressions can be exploited as a classroom resource in different ways. For example:

1. They can be projected as an OHT or placed on the desk as a handout in front of pairs or groups of students during performance of the activity to which they relate. This might make the expressions more prominent and accessible to students as they speak, and encourage their use.

2. They can be handed to one or two students who are to act as group observers during discussion activities. The task of the observers is to monitor the discussion and tick those expressions which are used and the names of the students who use them. The observer can then show the completed sheet to the group as part of post-discussion feedback or to individual students as feedback on their use or non-use of the language.

3. They can be cut into strips and distributed to students prior to the discussion or activity they relate to. Each student has a complete set of expressions. To encourage students to use the expressions, they are asked to set the ones aside which they use during the activity. These can then be 'counted' at the end of the activity. Different variations on this are possible.

4. They can be cut into strips and distributed to pairs or groups of students, who then need to categorize the expressions according to their function. For example, the expressions in the *useful language* box in Unit 4 on clarifying and confirming understanding can be categorized into the three groups given in the box *(confirming understanding as a listener, checking understanding as a speaker* and *showing that you do not understand)*. The category headings can be put on the board for students to refer to.

This type of categorization can be done when the language is originally presented or as a review later on.

Photocopiable

Useful language: Reporting back

Our group thought the most controversial point was …

Point X provoked the most discussion.

Point X was the most controversial point.

There was some disagreement about point X.

Some people felt …

Most of the group agreed …

Others disagreed …

Useful language: Agreeing and disagreeing

Absolutely. I totally agree.

Yes, that's true, but …

I'm not sure I agree with you there.

I agree up to a point, but …

Not necessarily.

That's a very good point.

Useful language: Signpost expressions (see also Appendix 1 in the Course Book)

There are five main that we consider important for successful study.

Our first point is …

Next, we have put …

Moving onto our third point …

Fourthly, we think …

And finally, our last point is …

Unit 2

Useful language: Comparing perspectives

From (a teacher's) perspective, …

From the point of view of (the parents), …

If I were (the headteacher of the child's school), I'd probably feel that …

(The child psychologist) would argue that …

Useful language: Summarizing a discussion

Summing up your position

We finally all agreed that …

After much consideration, we decided that …

All things considered, we felt that …

On balance, we felt that …

We couldn't reach agreement on this issue. Some of us felt that …, whilst others …

Recognizing strong arguments against your position

It's true that …

We recognized that …

We're fully aware that …

One has to acknowledge that …

Qualifying your position

This action should only be taken if …

So, although we agreed with the statement, we stressed that …

Useful language: Chairing a discussion

Getting started

Shall we begin?

Today, we're looking at the following question/topic …

Who would like to begin?

Clarification

So what you mean is …

If I've understood you correctly …

Managing contributions

Thanks, Pete, for your contribution …

OK, Pete, would anyone else like to comment?

Concluding

So, to sum up …

We're running out of time, so …

Does anyone want to make a final point?

Have I forgotten anything?

Unit 3

Useful language: Referring to an article

It provides …

This article deals with …

The article reports that …

It refers to …

The article also gives statistics from …

According to the article, …

The article then goes on to say that …

The article argues that …

It quotes …

The article reports on …

It doesn't mention …

Useful language: Exchanging opinions

Asking for opinions

What are your views on this issue?

Do you agree?

Presenting your own opinion

Well, I think …

It seems to me that …

In my view, …

Photocopiable

Countering the other person's opinion

I take your point, but …

I understand what you're saying, but …

Well, I'm not sure if that's quite true …

But surely …

Unit 4

Useful language: Clarifying and confirming understanding

Confirming understanding as a listener

So what you're saying is …

So in your view …

If I understand you correctly, you're saying …

Checking understanding as a speaker

Do you understand what I mean?

Do you follow what I am saying?

Am I making sense?

Showing that you do not understand

I'm not sure I understand what you mean.

I didn't quite follow you. Could you explain that point again, please?

Could you repeat that, please?

Unit 5

Useful language: Referring to data

This graph gives information about …

This line here shows …

This chart describes …

As these figures illustrate, …

This chart clearly shows that …

Photocopiable

Useful language: Referring to other speakers

When you say ... do you mean that ...?

As you said, ...

You made an interesting point about ...

Following on from that point, ...

Regarding what you say about ...

Can I also pick up on your point about ...?

Those are fair arguments.

You make the point that ...

As I said before, ...

Unit 7

Useful language: Taking your turn

You want to make a point that is relevant at this moment in the discussion. You need to enter the discussion politely, but firmly:

Can I just come in here?

You want to make a point, but the discussion moves on before you can contribute or finish. You can still make your point later:

To go back to my earlier point, ...

Coming back to what John said earlier, ...

I think I agree with the point you made earlier, Anne.

You start speaking at the same moment as another student. Both of you stop to let the other speak. It is polite to offer each other the chance to continue:

A: Sorry, carry on.

B: No, go ahead.

A: Thanks. I think ... [A makes his/her point and then invites B to speak] Sorry, you were going to say ...

B: Yes, I think ...

You notice that a quiet student is trying to speak, but other students keep speaking first. You can help the quiet student to get the attention of the group:

I think David has been trying to make a point.

David, did you want to make a point?

Photocopiable

Unit 8

Useful language: Expressing quantity

Most Nearly all		of those interviewed/questioned … of the subjects … of the respondents …	reported/ stated/ claimed that …
Approximately Approaching Just under Just over	half a third 50 per cent		

Unit 9

Useful language: Expressing doubt and belief

I don't believe in this/in these!

They don't exist.

It can't possibly be true …

It might be true …

There might be something in it …

I believe it does work.

I believe it might work.

Photocopiable

Appendix 2: Miscellaneous teacher's forms

Appendix 2a

(Gapped version of the transcript for Unit 1 Ex 3.3)

1 A: If you want to succeed at university, you really need to manage your time well.
   B: _____, because otherwise you will fall behind.

2 A: It's important to do a lot of reading around before you choose a focus for your essays.
   B: _____ you need to limit the amount you read.

3 A: The best time to revise for exams is just before the exam, when the pressure is on.
   B: _____. Many people can't think clearly under pressure.

4 A: The same study skills are necessary on both undergraduate and postgraduate courses.
   B: _____ postgraduates probably need more developed research skills.

5 A: If you've completed an academic course in one country, you should be able to cope with a course in another country.
   B: _____. There are different academic cultures in different countries. You may have to learn a new approach to studying.

6 A: People have different learning styles. It helps you learn more quickly if you're aware of how you learn best.
   B: _____. It can really help you to study more efficiently if you understand your own strengths and weaknesses.

Appendix 2b: Presentation assessment (alternative form)

Name of presenter: _____

	1	2	3	4	5
Pronunciation					
Intonation					
Volume					
Speed					
Eye contact					

1 = poor
5 = very good

Other comments:

Photocopiable

Appendix 2c: Presentation assessment – Teacher feedback

Name:

Title:

	Needs improvement	Quite good	Good	Very good	Excellent
Pronunciation (sounds, stress, intonation)					
Delivery (volume, speed)					
Eye contact					
Accuracy of language					
Range of language					
Use of signpost expressions					
Use of visual aids					
Use of notes					
Organization of ideas					
Level of detail					

Overall comments:

Feedback on language (grammar, vocabulary, pronunciation):

Teacher:

Appendix 2d: Presentation assessment – Teacher feedback

Name of presenter: _____

Was the topic clearly identified at the beginning?	Yes / No
Were the main points of the article clearly explained?	Yes / No
Did the presenter give their own views on the article?	Yes / No
Did the presenter explain the meaning of any difficult or technical words?	Yes / No

Pronunciation of sounds and words	not clear / reasonably clear / clear / very clear
Intonation	not varied / quite varied / varied
Volume	too quiet / appropriate
Speed	too fast / too slow / appropriate
Eye contact	none / too little / reasonable / good / very good
Visual aid	not helpful / quite helpful / very helpful

Comments:

Teacher:

Prison is the most effective way of dealing with young offenders

Definition of prison:
a place of detention as a means of:
- punishing offenders
- protecting the public
- deterring people from re-offending
- rehabilitating offenders

Definition of young offenders:
- criminals aged 15–21

The alternatives to prison for young offenders are:
- electronic tagging
- community service
- fines
- punishment of parents (fines, prison)
- curfews
- banning orders

Photocopiable

Appendix 2f

Model 1: OHT 1.2

Reasons why prison is the most effective solution

- It protects the community

- It reduces fear in the community

- It reduces the costs caused by vandalism

- It protects young people from being drawn into crime

- It breaks up gangs

- Tough punishment at a young age prevents further crimes from being committed

Photocopiable

Road development is more important than environmental protection

Definition of road development:

- building new roads
- improving existing roads

Definition of environmental protection:
saving trees, plants, animals by:

- leaving the land to natural conditions
- creating protected areas

Reasons why road development is needed:

- roads are too congested
- air and noise pollution
- drivers get stressed
- more accidents
- delays
- businesses lose money
- country will become less competitive

Model 2: OHT 2.2

Reasons people do not like road development

- 'green land' is replaced by concrete

- historical places are destroyed

- some people's home life is disturbed

Appendix 2i: Assessing seminar leader's role – Teacher feedback

Name:

Date:

Topic:

1 Was the seminar topic appropriate? (e.g., a topic of interest to the group, and one they could participate in?)	Yes / No Please comment
2 Did the seminar leader give enough information about the topic in the beginning?	Yes / No Please comment
3 Did the leader manage the seminar successfully? – keep the discussion going? – allow everyone the opportunity to speak? – ensure one individual did not dominate?	Yes / No Please comment
4 In what ways could the seminar discussion have been improved?	Please comment
5 Language areas to work on:	Pronunciation Grammar

Teacher:

Appendix 2j: Assessing seminar leader's role – Teacher feedback

(alternative feedback form)

Name:
Date:
Topic:

Presentation of seminar topic	
Management of seminar	
Language and pronunciation	
Overall comments	

Teacher:

Photocopiable

Copy your score for each question onto the answer grid below (NOTE: the numbers are NOT in sequence) and then add the scores in each vertical column.

1	2	3	4	5	6	7	8	9
15	12	14	10	18	11	17	16	13
25	23	21	20	27	24	26	22	19
30	36	28	29	31	33	35	32	34
38	43	45	39	41	42	37	44	40

Now add the score in each vertical column and insert the totals below.

MR	PI	ME	EX	CR	AF	AU	SE	ST

Source: © Garrat, B. & Frances, D. (1994) *Managing Your Own Career*. London: HarperCollins

Scoring

Career Drivers, according to Bob Garrat & Dave Francis (1994), give us energy and direction in pursuing our goals. They are not usually intellectual decisions but powerful internal imperatives. If you are not in tune with your own 'drivers' you may well feel de-motivated and unfulfilled. Are you, for example, influenced by someone else's expectations?

What are your highest scores? The most important thing is to find out which drivers influence you the most. You might have one or two that stand clear above the others – perhaps a main one and a subsidiary (or subsidiaries) or one or two that are broadly equal in influence.

If the driver(s) suggested by the exercise feel wrong to you, decide which you think yours is. You are the expert. But are you sure?

Francis's nine key drivers are:

MR   Material rewards – seeking possessions, wealth and a high standard of living.

PI   Power and influence – seeking to be in control of people and resources. Being in a position to make decisions, affect policies. Someone with this driver might be uncomfortable in a subordinate position but would flourish when they achieved a measure of power.

ME   Search for meaning – seeking to do things which are believed to be valuable for their own sake. ME people will look to satisfy their moral, emotional or spiritual values and will work for things they perceive to be more important than self.

EX   Expertise – seeking a high level of accomplishment in a specialized field.

CR   Creativity – seeking to innovate and be identified with original output. CRs prize originality; whether artistic or entrepreneurial. They often like working alone or in small teams.

AF   Affiliation – seeking nourishing relationships with others at work. Sometimes the job itself is not so important so long as they feel close and bond with colleagues.

AU   Autonomy – seeking to be independent and able to make key decisions for oneself. Usually hate bureaucracy, rules and constraints and strive to make their own choices.

SE   Security – seeking solid and predictable future. Want to feel unstressed about the future. Often enjoy working in well-known organizations.

ST   Status – seeking to be recognized, admired and respected. Often enjoy being a member of special groups. Not necessarily related to social class: for example someone could have status as a fashion leader.

Advice for international students from Speaker 1 (Gulin)

Cultural differences
Accept that these will exist.
Be tolerant of them, so that you can work with other students.
Expect similar acceptance and tolerance from them.

Study groups
Select students who live near you and who have a similar approach to study.
Be flexible in cooperating with them.

Tutor
Establish what kind of support you are entitled to (try reading the departmental handbook).
But remember that tutors vary: work out the most effective approach with your particular tutor.
Prepare for meetings so as to avoid wasting time: list points in advance in your order of priority.

Facilities on campus
Explore campus early on, to locate facilities (e.g., libraries, advisory services, Students' Union).
In the library, familiarize yourself with sections likely to be relevant to your studies. Enquire about specialist collections.
Make use of advisory services, e.g., consult Applied Statistics advisory service early on about the design of an experimental project.
Make use of the Students' Union – it is run by students for students. You can contact the Overseas Students' Committee, who have experience of your situation and want to improve it. The Union is also valuable as an information centre (about items for sale, accommodation to share, activities to take part in). The club activities (e.g., chess, mountaineering) are a good way to unwind, and to socialize with a wide range of students, both home and international.

Style of lecture
Be prepared for a lecture style in which contributions from the audience are often invited.
Practise so that you can join in. Do not discuss privately during lectures.

Approaching your course
See the course as a whole from the start: what is the most important part of it in terms of assessment and learning? If there is a dissertation, jot down ideas for it from early on in the course.

Advice for international students from Speaker 2 (Chris)

Tutors
Make full use of them.
Find out early on at what times they will be available for tutorial appointments.
Don't be shy about approaching them with questions. If you have a serious problem, report it to your tutor immediately.
If you don't have a personal tutor, take questions and problems to the lecturer instead.

Photocopiable

Reading
Be selective.
Ask the tutor to prioritize if necessary.

Study resources
At the library, make use of the recall system.
Talk your assignments over with fellow students: your initial ideas, your progress, difficulties you experience.
Try forming a study group, to work for an assignment or an exam. Select people who live conveniently nearby and with whom you can work easily. Studying in this way can be more enjoyable and more efficient (the workload is shared, and problems are clarified through discussion), and it gives you practice in expressing yourself.

Choosing options
Choose according to subject, not according to who is offering the option. An option in which you are genuinely interested is a better source of motivating topics for a dissertation.

Dissertation or long essay
Draft a proposal and seek a meeting early on to discuss it with your tutor.
Draw up a work schedule, with a reasonable deadline for each successive stage of the project. This is good for morale, as it makes the project seem manageable and gives you a sense of progress.

Photocopiable